REVEALING ANTIQUITY 22

G. W. BOWERSOCK, GENERAL EDITOR

GREEK MODELS
of MIND and SELF

A. A. Long

Harvard University Press

Cambridge, Massachusetts
London, England

2015

Copyright © 2015
by the President and Fellows of Harvard College

ALL RIGHTS RESERVED

Second Printing

Library of Congress Cataloging-in-Publication Data

Long, A. A.
Greek models of mind and self / Anthony A Long. — First [edition].
pages cm. — (Revealing antiquity ; 22)
Includes bibliographical references and index.
ISBN 978-0-674-72903-2 (alk. paper)
1. Mind and body 2. Philosophy of mind. 3. Self
(Philosophy) 4. Soul. 5. Philosophy, Ancient. I. Title.
B105.M53L66 2014
128.0938—dc23   2014009937

For Monique, as before

CONTENTS

Preface	ix
Translations and Citations	xv
Introduction	1
1. Psychosomatic Identity	15
2. Intimations of Immortality	51
3. Bodies, Souls, and the Perils of Persuasion	88
4. The Politicized Soul and the Rule of Reason	125
5. Rationality, Divinity, Happiness, Autonomy	162
Epilogue	198
Ancient Authors and Thinkers	203
Notes	207
Index	219

PREFACE

THIS BOOK IS based on lectures that I gave at Renmin University, Beijing, in May 2012. The university had recently established a biennial series of six master classes on ancient philosophy, and I had the great honor to be invited to deliver the second set of these. This was my first visit to the People's Republic of China. It was a thrill to have the opportunity of sharing my enthusiasm for Greek thought with the scholars and students of Renmin, and also with audiences at other Chinese universities, including Zhejiang, Fudan, and the University of Shanghai.

I drafted my lectures specifically for these occasions, but their topic, ancient Greek models of mind and self, has engaged me closely throughout my life as a teacher and scholar. Decades ago I undertook to write a book with this title for Harvard University Press. Over the years I published a large number of

PREFACE

articles on the subject in specialist journals, but the book itself eluded me. More than once I started to fulfill my old contract, but the complexity and scope of the subject were too daunting for me to complete the project. I had always wanted to present the material in ways that could engage a general audience, but successful books of that kind are much harder to write than learned monographs where an author can assume a good deal of background knowledge.

Renmin University's invitation gave me the opportunity and the incentive to try to overcome these scruples, and to honor my long-overdue obligations to Harvard University Press. This book is the result. It is a very small production, much smaller than I had projected years ago. It would be possible to write large volumes on each of my chapters' topics, and be equally expansive on related themes that I barely mention. But the smallness of the book may contribute, I hope, to its effectiveness. I have written it not for scholars but for anyone who is curious to explore the Greek genealogy of our western and, I dare say, cross-cultural language and thought about the mind and the self. I have written the book, moreover, not as a comprehensive survey of the field, but rather as a set of studies of the five topics indicated in my chapter headings. This selectivity will, I trust, give

PREFACE

readers new to the material sufficient detail and depth to make their own explorations with the help of the further readings I supply. A Chinese-language version of the book will be published by Peking University Press.

Many ancient authors, poets as well as philosophers, make their appearance here. Three of these predominate. They are Homer, Plato, and Epictetus, comprising ancient Greece's earliest and greatest poet, the culture's greatest philosopher, and the most accessible of Stoic philosophers, who spent his early life as a Roman slave. Chronologically the book ranges over a period of close to a millennium, but chronology and historical change are not my main focus. As I explain in the Introduction, what principally interest me are not scientific facts about the mind, supposing such truths to be accessible and demonstrable, but salient ways of describing and prescribing the way we experience, or might like to experience, the world and ourselves. The Greeks did not "discover" the mind, but they made a huge contribution to formulating the language and concepts of mind. That pertains, or so I will argue, no less to the epic poetry of Homer than it does to the explicit theories of Plato, Epictetus, and others. My conclusion, if such a grand word is applicable to so small a book, is a recommendation to assess the mind models not comparatively, as if one model gets it right and the others not, but experientially, so as to judge their effectiveness at capturing and illuminating our own self-understanding and aspirations.

My warm thanks are due to many people, far more than I can name here. I should first mention Dr. Wei Liu of Renmin University. He masterminded my visit to Beijing and elsewhere in China, shepherding my wife and myself with extraordinary kindness. Among other Renmin scholars I am especially grateful to Professor Han Donghui, Associate Dean of the School of Philosophy, who issued my official invitation to give the master classes. Turning now to this book itself and to Harvard University Press, I thank Glen Bowersock for inviting me so long ago to contribute a volume to his Revealing Antiquity series. He could have nagged me over the years. Instead, he has generously welcomed the book's belated inclusion in his series. The original suggestion for the book came from a good friend, Patricia Williams, who was then working as an editor for Harvard University Press. She was succeeded by Peg Fulton. Peg did all she could to revive my interest in this project when it flagged. Lindsay Waters, Executive Editor for the Humanities at the Press, encouraged me to publish

PREFACE

the lectures in this form. His interest in the work has been critical to my completing it, and I am also very thankful to Lindsay's editorial assistant, Shan Wang, for moving the project along. The two scholars who read my typescript for the Press sent me comments that have been extremely helpful in the process of turning the lectures into a book. I am also grateful to my copy editor, Karen Wise, whose queries and suggestions were always appropriate and frequently accepted.

Rather than generate a long list of scholarly helpers, which would be bound to fall badly short, I want to pay homage to three exceptional people, now alas deceased, to whom I feel especially indebted. David Furley, who introduced me to Greek philosophy at University College London, was an outstanding teacher. In writing this book I have constantly remembered his instruction to write a paper on Plato's psychology without mentioning the word *soul*. When I joined the Berkeley faculty in 1983, it was very much with the support of Tom Rosenmeyer. He believed in this book, and I always benefited from his advice and example. Bernard Williams, during his all too brief time on the Berkeley faculty, was a wonderfully stimulating friend. My approach to Homer has much in common with his work. I am grateful to

PREFACE

fellowship support I have received, especially as a member of the Wissenschaftskolleg zu Berlin in 1991–1992, and as holder of a President's Research Fellowship in the Humanities, of the University of California, in 1999–2000.

Turning to more recent times, I want to thank the many graduate students at Berkeley who have participated in seminars I have given over many years on topics related to this book. One of my current students, Derin McLeod, has helped me to compile some of the further readings I attach to the ends of chapters. Appropriately, perhaps, I applied finishing touches to the typescript in an East Asian context, as Distinguished Visiting Professor of Philosophy at the University of Hong Kong in the fall of 2013. At the final stage, Andrea Nightingale, with her inimitable insight, drew attention to some necessary adjustments.

My greatest thanks, as always, go to my wife, Monique. She has been a magnificent companion and support whenever and wherever I needed it most.

TRANSLATIONS AND CITATIONS

UNLESS STATED otherwise, the translations from Greek authors are my own. References to them are in the standard form of book number, followed by line or section number. The following modern book is cited in abbreviated form:

LS *Hellenistic Philosophers* = A. A. Long and D. N. Sedley, *The Hellenistic Philosophers,* vol. 1: *Translations of the Principal Sources, with Philosophical Commentary* (Cambridge, 1987).

INTRODUCTION

THE FIRST PREMISE of this book is that understanding our selves—our natures, capacities, and possibilities—is the hardest thing in the world and yet endlessly fascinating because it cannot be finally settled by empirical research. There are no facts to decide, once and for all, whether the mind is part of the body, or whether it is a spiritual substance, or an epiphenomenon of the brain. We still do not know, in a scientific sense, what consciousness is. My second premise is that we can continue to discover aspects of our human possibilities or aspirations by means of the Greek material I want to explore. I don't mean that we can discover these things, in the way we are adding every day to scientific knowledge about the brain's neurons and synapses. What I mean is that we can enlarge and enrich experience by recognizing how Greek authors, prior to modern science, represented the thing that is both closest to us and yet is still, in some sense, quite mysterious—our own essence as a human self. Many of their ideas are utterly remote from the individualistic and secular contexts of our body-centered market capitalism. That is all the more reason, or so I believe, for recovering these models of mind, irrespective of whether we can accommodate such thinking to modernity.

Intellectual historians have frequently taken themselves to be studying the *development* of concepts and ideas. Eduard Zeller, the great German historian of Greek philosophy, actually entitled his six-volume work *The Philosophy of the Greeks in Its Historical Development*.[1] A development is an unfolding, a growth, an evolution, a becoming clear or evident, an improvement or progress rather than a regression. Zeller approached the history of philosophy under the strong influence of Hegel, who understood human history as precisely a development in these senses, albeit a story that could involve intermittent descents as well as rises. This progressivist approach in the humanities, as distinct from the way we regard the physical sciences, is no longer fashionable. Nevertheless, because our experience throughout life follows the forward arrow of time, we can hardly avoid a tendency to think of the present as superseding the past, with the future promising new and different (if not better) vistas.

INTRODUCTION

The developmental outlook is difficult to set aside. It is particularly treacherous, however, if it inclines interpreters to treat the subject matter of this book as something that evolves in increasingly clear and definite and superior ways. Mind, self, and human identity are always present to us, and precisely for that reason, they are exceptionally difficult to discern independently from our particular cultural and subjective perspectives. It has often been supposed that early Greek notions of these things are confused or unclear or primitive when compared with the explicit formulations made by the classical philosophers Plato and Aristotle. Viewed in this way, Homer, who composed his epic poetry some three or four centuries earlier, either lacked a coherent understanding of our mental and bodily constitution or had a muddled grasp of the psychology that Plato and Aristotle would later formulate with clarity.

In this book I strongly resist the notion that ideas about mind or self develop in the linear way that is supposed by taking Homer to be primitive and taking Plato, by comparison, to be advanced. Homer's psychology, the subject of my first chapter, is implicit rather than explicit; the models that it betokens are there for us to detect rather than laid out for our inspection. But this is just to say that Homer was a supremely creative author of lifelike and imaginative narratives as distinct from being a theoretician and philosopher. Some things that Homer says, in fact some of his terminology, exactly anticipate Plato. Where they differ is neither to Homer's detriment nor to Plato's credit, nor again, by the same token, do such differences give Homer an edge over Plato. Any such ranking would be absurd. My presupposition, throughout this book, is that the mind modeling I will discuss, differing greatly among authors though it does, is consistently appropriate to their specific genre and purpose. At issue here are not facts, such as our biochemical structure or our brain cells, but linguistic and conceptual attempts to identify and understand the threads of our emotional, reflective, and purposive life, in order for us to make sense of living in the world. To set the scene accordingly, I begin the book by juxtaposing the Platonist Plotinus, one of antiquity's latest, greatest, and most abstract thinkers, with Homer. If this conflation of history seems strange and unwarranted, just read on.

The poems of Homer, untouched by philosophical or scientific theory, exhibit a cardiovascular model of the mind. Homer's epic diction is immensely rich in its resources to convey felt experience—fear, anger, the rush of energy, the impact of a weapon on flesh. Homer has a range of words to name the heart or the chest, where we actually do feel these things.[2] I call this first chapter "Psychosomatic Identity" because Homer, unlike the Greek philosophers, draws no binary distinction, in his descriptions of human behavior, between body and mind or between body and soul. When and why did that hoary distinction first emerge? Even if we dismiss the distinction today as "folk psychology," or as a mere *façon de parler* with no scientific foundation, it is still alive and well. That should not surprise us. Whatever our scientific views may be, we continue to speak and think with these categories. The mind may be as physical, in its underpinnings and location, as our heart and our lungs, but we do not experience it that way. Our makeup consists of a body and a mind, or so we find it convenient to think and say in everyday life.

If all this seems obvious and natural, that is not the case in the Homeric *Iliad* and *Odyssey*. Hence their great interest for this book's topic. The poems of Homer present human behavior with incomparable power and intensity, but their author does not bifurcate his characters into bodies and minds, or bodies and souls. He employs the words that later authors

GREEK MODELS OF MIND AND SELF

used to talk that way, but his model for the structure or identity of his characters is unitary rather than binary. These figures have bodies, of course, and they have minds; they have limbs and organs; they think and they feel, intensely and with wonderful realism. But Homer's men and women, rather than being represented as embodied minds or as having a mind that is distinct from the body, are what I call psychosomatic wholes. They are infused throughout with life. Where they think and feel, and what they think and feel with, are as much parts of their general makeup as are their hearts and their guts. These features of Homeric persons do not, to repeat, imply that they are bodiless or mindless. It is just that Homer, or rather Homer's linguistic culture, saw no need to carve people up into two distinct entities or dimensions.

How then, and why did that happen? To put the question another way, why did subsequent Greek thinkers take it to be axiomatic, as they did, that human identity and selfhood presuppose a radical difference between the body and the mind? Or, to pose the question more precisely in Greek terms, why did they posit the *psyche* or soul as the center of consciousness and as the core of a human identity or character? I conclude my first chapter by returning to

INTRODUCTION

Platonic dualism. The relationship between Platonists and Homer, which includes common ground as well as antithesis, sets up my context for the three ensuing chapters.

Chapter 2, "Intimations of Immortality," continues my earlier discussion of Homer and concludes with two of the earliest Greek philosophers, Empedocles and Heraclitus. The starting point for my discussion is Homer's emphasis on human mortality and Plato's remarkable ideas about the soul's preexistence and survival. Was Plato simply dreaming, or did he have cultural support for this gigantic disagreement with Greece's most authoritative text? To support the second alternative, I draw upon mythological material concerning gods and humans in the poetry of Hesiod, who was a near contemporary of Homer, and explore ideas about the postmortem destiny of souls presented by the fifth-century poet Pindar. I ask what cultural factors may have encouraged belief in an afterlife. Homeric characters are essentially mortal. They are survived by nothing more substantial than a ghost. If, on the other hand, human identity includes the presumption that an individual can survive death, the already living person requires something other than its mortal coil to be the constant and continuing center of itself, now and hereafter. In that case are human beings simply human or are they related to divinity—or are they even fallen gods? Empedocles described the continuing self not as a *psyche* but as a *daimon,* a divine spirit. Thinkers who came after him drew on that word to designate the human mind and its rationality, as we shall see in Chapters 4 and 5. Here again, in this supreme elevation of our intellectual powers, we find a remarkable difference from the Homeric outlook. It is a further sign of how our own modeling of the mind may be closer in some respects to Greek epic poetry than to Greek philosophy.

Are life and death, or mortality and immortality, polar opposites, or are they two sides of a continuum? In a series of cryptic statements that raise such questions, Heraclitus challenged inquiry into the deepest reaches of selfhood. Rather than looking to *psyche* as the bearer of moral identity and postmortem destiny (as we find in Pindar), Heraclitus formulated startlingly new assertions about the physical composition and power of the human *psyche* and about its function as the locus of mind and self.

By the end of the fifth century BCE, Greek authors, when talking about human nature, had begun to compare and contrast *psyche* with what has become the standard word for body *(soma),* meaning

INTRODUCTION

our physical frame. When and why that comparison and antithesis became common linguistic practice we cannot say with any precision. We know it best and most influentially from the dialogues of Plato. Socrates (the historical figure, not just Plato's character) probably urged his contemporaries to cultivate their souls rather than their bodies, as Plato represents him as doing. It would be difficult, if not impossible, to translate that thought into Homeric Greek. Owing to Plato's philosophical depth and influence, we may be tempted into taking his accounts of the soul's excellence and capacity for self-control and intellectual integrity to be the truth of the matter, or at least generally acceptable to his culture, in its recognition of the mind's difference from the body.

Actually, Plato's account of the *psyche,* far from being "natural" or self-evident, would still have seemed highly controversial and implausible to many Athenians, especially those who recognized the power of demagogues to manipulate mass audiences. In my third chapter, "Bodies, Souls, and the Perils of Persuasion," I argue that the rhetorician Gorgias was a major catalyst in Plato's formative thinking and contrasts of soul and body. Gorgias argues that any audience can be manipulated by a supremely effective speaker.

GREEK MODELS OF MIND AND SELF

In writing about Helen of Troy, Gorgias repeatedly contrasts the strength of bodies and bodily beauty with the weakness of souls to resist persuasive speech. That goes in the opposite direction from Plato, or at least what Plato would have his readers believe. Plato's extreme dualism, by which he pits the powers and excellence of the philosophical soul against the demands of the body, cannot be accounted for in a few pages of a modern book. However, the rhetorician Gorgias enables us to identify an important line of its genealogy. I show how the dualistic model fits Plato's manifesto to defend philosophy (for which Socrates was his hero) against rhetoric. This chapter concludes with the dialogue *Phaedo,* where Plato sets the scene of Socrates's last mortal day, and I adjoin a brief comparison and contrast with later philosophical treatments of the soul's relation to the body.

In Chapter 4 I take up a topic that I adumbrated at the end of Chapter 1, namely, Plato's division of the soul into three parts, each of them supposedly a distinct source of motivation—appetitive, emotive, and calculative. This psychological model differs from that of the *Phaedo* by transferring the unruly influence of the body to appetitive urges that are situated within the soul itself. I entitle this chapter "The Politicized Soul and the Rule of Reason." Prior

INTRODUCTION

to Plato, or so I think, no Greek author had explicitly linked the notions of political functioning and good administration with *reason* or *reasoning.* Before Plato, moreover, the notions of reason and reasoning had barely begun to be theorized. Like the mind, of course, they are as old as our earliest forebears, but that does not mean that they were identified, labeled, and analyzed as such. Plato's philosophical predecessors, with the exception of Heraclitus and one or two instances elsewhere, are not explicit about reason (in Greek, *logos*). In this chapter I show how Plato turns to politics (asking the question "Who or what should rule and how?") in order to illuminate the structure and best functioning of the mind. His proposal in the *Republic,* that reason is naturally equipped to best govern both society and our individual selves, was a striking innovation in its time. Readers should ask themselves whether, or to what extent, Plato got it right. I conclude the chapter with comments on Plato's focus on reason's rule beyond the context of politics and on his influence on Aristotle's philosophy of mind.

Having just presented weighty statements from Plato and Aristotle concerning the divinity or quasi-divinity of the mind, in the book's fifth and final chapter I ask what that attribute signified in its ancient contexts and what, if anything, it might still mean for us. I myself have no theistic inclinations or commitments, but as a historian I find the ancient philosophers' divinity of the mind not only fascinating but also central to understanding their deepest intuitions about the self. The notion is essential to understanding the interconnections between rationality, happiness, and autonomy as they saw these things. In the first part of the chapter I look at this theme in a generic fashion, linking Plato, Aristotle, Epicurus, and Stoicism. Then I pursue it with a close study of the Stoic philosophy of mind and self, drawing especially on the most accessible discourses composed by Epictetus for his young Roman students. Given the brevity and range of this book, I am well aware that these final remarks may strike some of my professional colleagues (if they read them) as incommensurate with anything that makes psychological sense in 2014. In that case, though, we must either accept a cognitive chasm between ourselves and the ancient philosophers or try, as I have done, to find ways of translating the "divinity" of mind into a metaphorical mode that can still provide us with insights into our own potentialities.

Throughout this book, I have attempted to hear the voice of the Greek thinkers and to engage them,

INTRODUCTION

in spite of their historical distance, in a meaningful conversation. This dialogical endeavor, which is how I try to teach the material, explains my largest omission. All the major philosophers, especially Aristotle, Epicurus, and the Stoics, have much to say about the physiological relation of the soul to the body. Why have I almost entirely bypassed this topic, after airing it in my first chapter on psychosomatic identity? Once the soul/body distinction became standard parlance among philosophers, they developed the language of mind in ways that are largely indifferent to the mind's physical constitution even if they thought that it was a part of the body. Whether the mind is an emergent property of atoms, as Epicurus proposed, or a function of the pneumatic material that energizes a living body, as the Stoics supposed, or an incorporeal entity, as in the Platonic tradition—irrespective of these great differences, the ancient models of mind are alike in their main agenda. Their physiology or metaphysics of the mind can tell us little or nothing about our mental experience today. But the concepts of mind they deployed and refined—rationality, irrationality, desire, passion, motivation, practical and theoretical thought—apply across the board and overstep history. They are our concepts now, and to that extent we still have Greek models of mind.

Further Reading

Gill, C. (1996), *Personality in Greek Epic, Tragedy, and Philosophy: The Self in Dialogue* (Oxford).

Nightingale, A., and Sedley, D. (2010), eds., *Ancient Models of Mind: Studies in Human and Divine Rationality* (Cambridge, UK). This volume, largely composed by my former students, offers detailed studies of Plato, Aristotle, Stoicism, and Plotinus.

Snell, B. (1953), *The Discovery of the Mind: The Greek Origins of European Thought;* translation of *Die Entdeckung des Geistes,* 2nd ed. (Göttingen, 1948) by T. G. Rosenmeyer (Oxford).

Sorabji, R. (2006), *Self: Ancient and Modern Insights about Individuality, Life, and Death* (Oxford).

Williams, B. (2008), *Shame and Necessity,* 2nd ed. (Berkeley/Los Angeles).

1

PSYCHOSOMATIC IDENTITY

WHAT IS THE nature of human beings? According to Plotinus, who asked this question, we humans live our lives simultaneously at two quite distinct levels.[1] One of these levels is obvious to everyone and not in doubt, no matter how we explain the details of human life. This obvious life is our everyday embodied experience, with our immediate desires, hopes, fears, thoughts, memories, expectations, and hourly activities. This is a life or being *in time* that everybody knows directly. The other level of life, according to Plotinus, is unobvious because it is everlasting and not accessible to normal consciousness. This other level, unlike the first one, is not our immediate, embodied experience. It is a purely intellectual life that consists timelessly in the contemplation of eternal truths. Plotinus infers that we have this further life on the basis of purely theoretical,

GREEK MODELS OF MIND AND SELF

nonempirical considerations that have to do with understanding how and why there can be truths, as there are in mathematics, that never change and that transcend all particular points of view. What Plotinus calls the "we" (or the human self) straddles two levels, making us, as he says, "amphibious" or double. According to this conception we live simultaneously in both a physical, bodily, material, and temporal dimension and in a spiritual, immaterial, and immortal realm. For Plotinus, human beings are fully themselves, fully experience what it is to be human, only at this higher incorporeal and intellectual level. According to him, we should try, here and now, to identify ourselves with the life of the everlasting intellect, letting go of the body and embodied consciousness as much as possible. Thus, to Plotinus, human nature is uncompromisingly dualistic, with body and mind essentially different things.

In this respect, as in so many other ways, the outlook of Plotinus is a complete contrast with the sensuous immediacy and concreteness of Greece's epic poet, Homer. When the *Iliad* and *Odyssey* were first written down in about 700 BCE, close to a thousand years before the birth of Plotinus, the two poems

PSYCHOSOMATIC IDENTITY

became at once the earliest and the greatest literary creations of ancient Greece. The heroes of these epics, Achilles and Odysseus, are intensely conscious of their present embodied and time-governed existence, and they are equally conscious of their social identity and high rank as warrior chieftains. These heroes have no inkling of a second level of timeless being, a higher intellectual and immortal level, such as Plotinus envisioned. For Achilles and Odysseus, what matters—as it continues to matter for all of us, nearly thirty centuries later—is how one fares here and now, in the succession of days, what one feels and what one desires, how one succeeds and where one fails. Achilles and Odysseus envision nothing like immortality or an amphibious self divided between body and mind. The life of the Homeric heroes is an intensely physical existence, and it will be completely and irrevocably over when they die. Indeed, one of Homer's most characteristic terms for human beings is "mortals" *(brotoi)* to contrast us with "immortals" *(athanatoi),* meaning gods. Yet, something of the Homeric human being will persist after death, something that Homer calls the *psyche.*

Is this *psyche* an entity or a nonentity? One is tempted to call it a nonentity because it is insubstantial and ghostly, a lifeless replica of the living person, consigned to inhabit Hades, the dark and gloomy underworld of shades. Yet, in spite of its insubstantiality, a Homeric *psyche* is not nothing: it is the ghost of someone in particular, someone who has already lived a particular embodied life. When Homeric persons *expire,* they breathe forth their *psyche* once and for all. The life that they have lived is finished, as shown by the corpse that the *psyche* leaves behind. So, at the beginning of the *Iliad* we are told that the shades *(psychai)* of countless warriors have been sent to Hades, leaving "themselves" (that is, their bodies) as carrion for dogs and birds.[2] Similarly, the shade of an unburied hero asks Odysseus to "bury me," where "me" refers to his corpse.[3] Here is a huge difference from Plotinus. In one of the greatest contrasts in intellectual history, the disembodied, ghostly, lifeless Homeric *psyche* will be transformed into the bearer of human life and identity at its truest, best, and most real, according to the Platonic tradition that Plotinus represents.

How did this happen? What shifts in human imagination and aspiration were at work in this remarkable transition from a body-centered being in time, with death as the end of actual human

PSYCHOSOMATIC IDENTITY

existence, to a spiritual, bodiless immortality as humanity's ultimate destiny? In this book, I will sketch some possible answers to these questions, but my goal is more analytical than it is historical. Rather than differentiating between Homer's Bronze Age culture and the late Roman Empire of Plotinus, I chiefly want to explore ideas that figure in a selection of Greek models of the self, starting with Homer and ending with Stoicism. My explorations will illustrate changes through time in the representation of human identity and selfhood, but I will also emphasize continuities and connections. Models of mind and selfhood, as observed in my Introduction, do not evolve in a tidy, linear path. Discarded concepts are sometimes revived or restructured, and every model, to be effective, must respond to the familiar, fundamental, and unchanging facts of subjective experience that transcend particular times, places, and cultures.

Plotinus himself provides a fascinating instance of the kind of continuity or connection I have in mind. In a famous passage from the *Odyssey* (11.601–2), the wandering hero, who gives his name to the epic, has a vision of the shades. At one point, describing his experience, he says:

> Next I saw the shade *(eidolon)* of mighty
> Hercules. But he himself takes delight in
> feasting with the immortal gods.

Plotinus comments (*Ennead* 1.1.12):

> Homer seems to separate Hercules from his
> mere image. He puts his image [or shade] in
> Hades, but Hercules himself among the gods;
> treating the hero as existing in the two realms
> at once, he gives us a twofold Hercules.

Here Plotinus updates Homeric mythology by interpreting it as an indication of his own dualistic system with its stark distinctions between soul or mind and body. Hercules, with Zeus as his father and Alcmene as his mother, had been traditionally perceived as a demigod—a composite of the human and the divine. This complex parentage explained how Hercules, the man, could die and pass to Hades as a shade, while his divine essence (what Homer calls "Hercules himself") joined the immortal gods. In this traditional story Plotinus saw the kernel of his own remarkable doctrine already described—the idea of an amphibious or bifurcated identity for everyone, divided between a mortal body and a higher self, a self that is everlasting and focused entirely on the life of the mind.

PSYCHOSOMATIC IDENTITY

When Greek philosophers reflected on ethics and theology, they found much to criticize and reject in Homer. But Homeric epic was so powerful and entrenched in Greek culture that no major philosopher could completely escape its influence, even a philosopher as abstract as Plotinus. Homer was an inescapable catalyst for all ancient philosophy, especially the notions of mind, self, and identity that I will discuss in this book. The poems of Homer not only set the stage for my project, they also provide recurrent themes for subsequent authors to develop, react against, or even appropriate, as we have just seen.

Homer, of course, did not pose abstract questions by asking, as Plotinus did directly, about the nature of human beings. The Homeric epics are intended to appeal to our emotions, not our intellects. But all Greek philosophers recognized Homer's richness for anyone's inquiry into the foundations of human identity. Around the time of Plotinus, an author (incorrectly identified as Plutarch) wrote a work on Homer in which he attempted to show, through a series of quotations, that Homer was the source of many specific doctrines of the Greek philosophers, especially Plato and Pythagoras, Aristotelians, and Stoics. Plutarch, as this author is called, makes much of his case by reading between the lines in ways that no one today would find convincing.[4] But his points are sometimes quite appropriate: he correctly notes that Stoic philosophers followed Homer in their account of the way life, breath, and heart are connected, and he shows that Homer could distinguish between fate and human responsibility for actions performed deliberately.[5] Plutarch goes quite astray in making Homer the source of *all* Greek philosophy, but he was right to align many Homeric contexts with ideas that subsequent philosophers had elaborated. One representative of this practice is Pyrrho, the eponymous founder of the version of skepticism called Pyrrhonism. We are told that Pyrrho had a habit of quoting Homeric passages to corroborate his own views on the uncertainty of everything.[6]

My interest in Homer, for the purpose of this chapter, is twofold. I want to illustrate and explain Homer's understanding of what we today call human physiology and psychology. In this part of the discussion my focus will be on objective features of human identity that belong to all human beings as a species. My second interest in Homer concerns notions that involve value and subjectivity, notions about the character and activity of an individual life—the things that make a life worthwhile or

PSYCHOSOMATIC IDENTITY

wretched, within or beyond an agent's control, intelligent or senseless. These notions pertain to Homeric contexts such as the anger of Agamemnon and Achilles, Odysseus's strategy in reclaiming his kingly position at Ithaca, and Penelope's steadfast refusal to accept rumors concerning Odysseus's death.

How do these two topics fit together—objective identity on the one hand and, on the other hand, subjectivity, individuality, and value? To answer this question I need to develop a theme that will be important throughout the book—the distinction already mentioned between body and soul or, to be more precise, the distinction often expressed in Greek between *soma* and *psyche,* which is the word that gave rise to our modern term *psychology.* Homer has both these words. As we saw in my opening remarks on Plotinus, Homer uses *psyche* to refer to the breath or spirit that leaves persons when they die and that persists as a ghost in Hades. *Soma* is Homer's word for the lifeless corpse that the *psyche* leaves behind. Do *living* humans, then, in Homer consist of a *soma* that contains a *psyche?* The answer may seem to be obviously yes. For how else could it make sense to say that death occurs when you breathe out your *psyche,* leaving a corpse behind? But the linguistic facts are a bit more complicated.[7]

GREEK MODELS OF MIND AND SELF

Many languages and cultures make sharp distinctions between the living body, meaning our anatomical parts and structure, and something they call the soul or the spirit. According to this distinction the soul or spirit is taken to be the source of embodied life and, in particular, the seat and cause of thought, feeling, and consciousness. Such a distinction between body and soul became the standard practice of ancient Greek philosophers, and it soon made its way into the general culture. We could accurately describe the Greek ethical tradition from Socrates onward as a focus on care of the soul as distinct from care of the body. As we shall see in later chapters, models of self and personal identity in Greek philosophy take a distinction between soul and body to be basic to an understanding of human nature in general and also to an understanding of the mental and moral differences between people. Many Greek philosophers (Aristotle is a partial exception) have what we may call a thing-like view of soul or *psyche*. In general, they assign a definite location within the body to *psyche*, sometimes by dividing it into specific parts. In so doing, they treat *psyche* in much the same way as we moderns do when we speak of the head or the brain.

We might expect that Homer anticipated this seemingly natural distinction, but most scholars say

PSYCHOSOMATIC IDENTITY

that he did not. The chief reason for their denial is that Homer does not speak of a living body or a living soul when he uses the words *soma* and *psyche*. He confines his use of these terms to contexts of death rather than life, with *soma* referring, as I have said, to the corpse, and *psyche* to the breath of life that people lose when they die. Thus at the beginning of the *Iliad* (in a passage cited above), we read that "the wrath of Achilles hurled countless sturdy *psychai* of heroes to Hades, and left the men *themselves* as carrion for dogs and birds." How, then, does Homer describe the nature of living persons?

In what follows we shall see that living persons in Homer are bodies through and through. Like the dead "men themselves" resulting from Achilles's anger, in Homer's conception the human identity is completely bodily or physical. Does this mean that Homer has no notion of the soul, or of a soul? This too is widely assumed. The assumption would be correct if the conception of a soul must be expressed by the single term *psyche,* as it generally is in Greek from the time of Plato. The assumption would also be correct if the conception of a soul must be of something immaterial, as it is for Plato and Plotinus. But both of these assumptions are false. *Psyche* is not the only word in Greek that signifies the cause of life, and the seat of thought, feeling, and consciousness. Furthermore, whether the soul (whatever its name) is material or immaterial became a subject of disagreement among ancient philosophers. Many of them, including Epicurus and the Stoic philosophers, took the soul to be as material as the body. The falsity of these two assumptions permits us to repeat the question. Does Homer, notwithstanding his body-centeredness, have a notion of the soul or of a soul, and does he have a word or words to signify that notion?

The answer is a strong affirmative. Homer has a very rich vocabulary for identifying the constituents of human beings. This vocabulary includes words for the external and internal parts of the body, words for the limbs or physical form in general, and words for the location and the instruments of thoughts and feelings, or for conscious life in general. Two of these latter words became standard in ancient philosophy—*nous* (spelled *noos* in Homeric Greek), commonly translated as mind or intellect, and *thumos,* commonly rendered as spirit or temper. In addition, Homer uses other words that refer directly to the heart or another internal organ for the location of thought and feeling, especially the words *phren* (or *phrenes*), *kradie,* and *etor.* Scholars have often wondered why Homer has these multiple words for referring to the location or instrument of human thought and feeling. Why does he not always use the same word, a word like *mind* or *soul* in English, or *Geist* or *Seele* in German?

This turns out to be an inappropriate question, for even in modern languages we vary our terminology in everyday speech. We may say "I had this in my mind," or "I had this in my head," or "I felt this in my heart," or "I had a sinking feeling in my stomach." When we use these different expressions, we are not implying some uncertainty about our mental and bodily apparatus. All these expressions signify a mental experience. Often we use just a personal pronoun and a verb, as in "I thought" or "I felt." At other times, for emphasis, we may use these more elaborate expressions, adding "in my head" or "in my heart." Homer is similar. His multiple words for the location or instrument of thought and feeling need not imply, as scholars have often supposed, that he lacked a unitary notion of what we may call mental experience. Rather, his wide range of words can be explained, to a great extent, by the fact that thinking and feeling are not localizable in the way that our limbs are. In addition, Homer needed to find a range of rhythmically distinct but roughly synonymous terms to fit the metrical requirements of hexameter verse.

GREEK MODELS OF MIND AND SELF

We may still be wondering what the Homeric *psyche* does for persons when they are alive. My answer to this question is that it too is probably ill framed. We are tempted to ask it because the *psyche* of later thinkers became the preferred name for the soul, as I have just characterized it, signifying the vital center of the entire person and incorporating what we more commonly today call mind, character, self, or personality, rather than soul. Once *psyche* had acquired these meanings, it provided numerous ways of thinking about human identity and selfhood that distinguish explicitly between bodily characteristics on the one hand and mental and moral features on the other hand. Just as people differ in physical size or weight or strength, so, by analogy, post-Homeric people were regularly taken to differ in the size, quality, or strength of their *psyche*. Hence Aristotle described his ideal person as *megalopsychos,* "great in soul" or, in idiomatic English, "high-minded," while one of Aristotle's words for an inferior person is the exact opposite—"small in soul" *(mikropsychos)*.[8] Just why the term *psyche* became the preferred term for the soul is an intriguing question that I will try to answer in Chapter 2. The crucial point for now is to recognize that its absence from Homer's psychological terminology does not imply that he has no concept of a soul.

PSYCHOSOMATIC IDENTITY

Homer's practice of using *soma* and *psyche* in contexts where a life is lost rather than lived has provoked enormous discussion. In particular it has prompted the idea that he was a conceptual primitive, an author who lacked the obvious realization that living persons consist of a unified body and a unified soul. Homer, it was once widely thought, treated his characters as a disunited assemblage of parts—body parts and mental parts—instead of viewing the characters as psychosomatic wholes or full-fledged selves. This influential interpretation of Homer, advanced by the German scholar Bruno Snell, has now been largely discredited.[9] As we read about the actions of Achilles or Odysseus, we immediately understand their credibility according to our own understanding of human behavior. At the same time, we recognize that these figures are Homeric heroes as distinct from modern persons. Above all, we need to accustom ourselves to read Homer in Homer's terms, lest we overlook some of his insights into human nature from a belief that he has missed out on the truth because he has not read Plato.

This was Snell's big mistake, great scholar though he was. Snell assumed that Homer did not fully understand human nature because he lacked Plato's sharp distinction between soul and body, a distinction

GREEK MODELS OF MIND AND SELF

that Snell took to be factually correct rather than the contestable theory that it actually is. Why and how Plato made that distinction is a fascinating question, which I will discuss at length in due course. For now I will make just three preliminary points about it.

First, the dramatists Aeschylus and Sophocles are similar to Homer in their reticence about dividing human beings dualistically into distinct entities called bodies and souls. In other words, if we take Homer to be primitive because he lacks this model of human nature, we need to say the same about these two tragedians, who were composing centuries later and close in date to Plato. Yet no one is tempted to find Aeschylus or Sophocles psychologically primitive. Second, Plato does not ignore Homeric language and thought concerning mind or soul. He sometimes draws on it directly and positively, as we shall see. The point on which Homer and Plato differ most radically concerns the postmortem destiny of the *psyche*. For Homer, as we have seen, there is no afterlife or immortality; the *psyche* that Homer's dying persons breathe forth is a mere ghost. For Plato, by radical contrast, the *psyche* is not only the essence of the living person, it is also something so distinct from the body that it can be judged, rewarded, punished, and

PSYCHOSOMATIC IDENTITY

reborn in a human or even a nonhuman body. My third point is an extension of what I have just said. Homer and Plato agree that death consists in the departure of the *psyche* from the body. If, like Homer, you suppose that nothing more than a ghost survives death, you will suppose that this event—the departure of the *psyche*—just means that the life has gone out of the person: the person has breathed his or her last, as we say. In that case, there is no reason to ask about the function of the *psyche* within the living body. To ask that question would be vacuous, like asking, "What's the function of being alive?" But if, like Plato, you suppose that the body is merely the container of yourself—that the essential you is not your body but the immortal soul within your body—then it is obviously pertinent to raise explicit questions about the body/soul relationship.

Homer's epic poems, to a significant extent, are about death or the threat of death. Mortality—the inevitability of a life's irrevocable end—is never absent from the *Iliad* and is often emphasized in the *Odyssey*. Yet, in spite of the pathos that the theme of mortality generates, Homer's epic poetry is much more prominently about life—indeed, an intense celebration of life. This celebration requires mortality as its antithetical adjunct. Homer delights in the vibrancy of every living moment. That moment may be something to embrace, like the love of Hector and Andromache, or it may be something to shrink from, like the intensity of Achilles's blood lust in revenge for Patroclus. At many junctures of his tales Homer invites our approval or disapproval of his personages, but his presentation of their lives transcends such judgments. His language is magnificently designed to enable us to enter and share fictive experiences, whether they involve a surge of energy, a deadly wound, a thoughtless impulse, a calculated choice, or pent-up emotion.

Here are two illustrations of my point. As I present them, readers will do well to remember the discredited theory of Homer's supposedly fragmented notions of the self and his supposed lack of an understanding that human beings are psychosomatic wholes. The god Poseidon, taking on the form of the seer Chalcas, has just exhorted the brothers Ajax to do their best to defend the Argive ships from an onslaught by Trojan Hector. I now translate (*Iliad* 13.61–79):

> The god filled them both with powerful
> strength *(menos);* he made their limbs agile,

their feet and their hands above.... [One of
the two Ajax brothers, recognizing that a god
has intervened, now comments to the other
one]: "Within myself the spirit *(thumos)* in my
chest is more eager to fight and wage war. My
feet below and my hands above are itching to
go." [His brother responds]: "It's just so for me,
too; my invincible hands around the spear are
itching to go; strength *(menos)* has welled up
in me, and below with both feet I am rushing
along."

An author could have expressed Poseidon's effects on the two warriors much more simply by saying, for instance, that the god filled them with fresh determination. Homer, too, could have expressed himself thus. Here, instead, he gives us a marvelously detailed and realistic anatomy of the feeling necessary for effective hand-to-hand combat—an injection of "strength," the response of "the spirit in the chest," and sensations in feet and in hands. In this description both body and mind (or soul) are present, but, rather than being distinct parts of each of the two brothers, they are conjoined, as expressed by saying "the spirit *in* my chest," just as spirit and chest are conjoined in real life. Is the spirit, as described here, part of the mind or part of the body? The question loses pertinence once we take this passage to be telling us what battle readiness feels like. It is neither in one's mind as such nor in one's body as such, but in one's chest, one's hands, and one's feet, all together. So battle readiness makes the person completely energized for combat.

The word translated as "spirit" is *thumos*. This is Homer's favorite word for referring to the conscious center of a person. Sometimes *thumos* is the subject of a sentence: it may desire, or urge, or think. Most interestingly, a Homeric hero may address his own *thumos*, and then ask, "Why has my *thumos* spoken to me thus?" We, too, sometimes say or think, "What do I have in mind?" or "Why did I say this to myself?" One is tempted to explain Homer's use of *thumos* in many contexts as a circumlocution for the personal pronoun, the use of "mind" or "spirit" instead of "I" or "myself." Interpretations of Homer's underlying patterns of thought must allow for his formulaic phraseology and the strictness of his metrical form, but we had better acknowledge that *thumos* is neither a pronoun nor simply equivalent to the word "I." The etymology of *thumos* tells us that its basic meaning is breath, and specifically, the breath of life. Hence, *thumos,* just like Homeric *psyche,* is breathed out when

PSYCHOSOMATIC IDENTITY

one dies. Can we, then, replace *thumos* in translation by a phrase like "life breath?" That is not good English. Hence translators typically translate *thumos* as heart or mind. In that case, though, we lose the distinctiveness of Homer's terminology, which refers neither to the anatomical heart nor to the cerebral head. *Thumos* here, I propose, stands for the Homeric soul, and it should be translated by "spirit." It stands for the Homeric soul not because the word *thumos* exactly signifies mind or heart or soul, as a modern speaker might utter any one of these words, but because life breath, energy, and feeling make us what we are as real persons. In Homer, *thumos* represents a person's mental and emotional identity or self, and by saying that I mean that is exactly what Homer wants *thumos* to signify, nothing more and nothing less.

Very often Homer combines mention of *thumos* with other "psychological" words, including *phren* (or *phrenes*), *stethos*, *etor*, and *kradie*. For instance, when Agamemnon insists on seizing the girl Briseis from Achilles, to whom she was assigned as his rightful war prize, Homer proceeds:

> Anguish came over Achilles, the heart *(etor)*
> within his shaggy chest went back and

> forth—should he draw the sharp sword from
> his thigh and kill Agamemnon, or end his rage,
> and tamp down his spirit *(thumos)*? While he
> rushed over these things in his lungs *(phrenes)*
> and spirit *(thumos)* and was drawing his great
> sword from its sheath, Athena arrived from
> heaven. (*Iliad* 1.188–93)

Here, as we have seen before, the mental and the physical are brought together, creating a wonderfully vivid picture of Achilles's distraught condition. What, though, are we to make of Homer's mental anatomy? He uses three words, *etor, phrenes,* and *thumos,* all of which appear to identify the internal location of Achilles's thoughts and emotions. Are these words synonymous, or do they pick out three different parts of Achilles? Actually, my translations "heart" and "lungs" are too precise to render the Homeric meaning with the charge that these words have in the original Greek. The words that I have so translated should not be taken in an anatomically exact way. Rather they express Homer's poetically varied intuition that the respiratory and cardiac parts of the body are the seat of a person's thoughts and feelings—in other words, what, to repeat my earlier point, we may safely call the Homeric soul.

To avoid unnecessary detail and technicality, I should say that such combinations ("heart *and* spirit" and so on) show that Homer takes *thumos* to be located within the region of the chest, exactly as we would expect from the notion that our vital principle is breath. Is *thumos*, then, a bodily organ? I suggest that this again is an inappropriate question. For Homer, *thumos* is the breathing vitality and consciousness of a living, human body. As such, it comprises mental abilities, emotional drives, and energizing powers. It is not a soul in Plato's sense of a single entity within us that is quite distinct from our bodily parts. It is not that because the Homeric *thumos* functions in conjunction with the other parts I mentioned; it is not set above them, nor does it organize them. Rather, the complex of *thumos*, along with these other parts, is what enables human beings to function, to say it again, as psychosomatic wholes.

The points I am making are brilliantly described by Michael Clarke in his book *Flesh and Spirit in the Songs of Homer*. I will summarize this part of my discussion with the following quotation from Clarke's work (p. 115):

> Because the oozing, flowing, billowing life of breath and the organs in the breast is dynamic, rather than static, it expresses the flow of mental life clearly and naturally, with at least as much depth and subtlety as does the language of mind in our own culture. Homer does not oppose mental life to the life of the body, but takes them as an undifferentiated whole. There is no "ghost in the machine": Homeric man does not *have* a mind, rather his thought and consciousness are as inseparable a part of his bodily life as are movement and metabolism.

Clarke's observations show that Homer's "psychological" terminology is excellently equipped for the composition of heroic poetry. Homer's characters are designed to derive their living identity from the vibrant breath that pulsates within them. Their life is for the here and the now. Once life breath *(thumos)* has left their limbs, it can no longer function as a self, such as the *thumos* that sometimes speaks and is spoken to. Homeric *thumos* is not the mental correlate of a dualistic conception of the person. It is not *the* soul as distinct from the body. But if we take soul to be the name for a human being's vital principle and the source of human agency, *thumos* clearly has soul-like features.

Plato recognized the soul-like features of Homeric *thumos*. In the earliest of the dialogues in which he divides the *psyche* into three distinct parts—calculative, appetitive, and spirited—Plato calls the spirited part *thumoeides,* a word that means literally "of *thumos* form."[10] Plato makes this psychological part responsible for our experiences of anger, shame, and ambition. The principal basis for his division of the soul is the fact that we sometimes find ourselves at the same time, or seemingly at the same time, subject to desires pro and contra the same thing. Thus we may experience a strong urge to satisfy an appetite while also recognizing that this objective is not in our longer-term interests and therefore something to be avoided because it is not a desire of reason. In addition to accounting for a self conflicted between the desire for immediate gratification and prudent restraint, Plato's division of the soul is also designed to accommodate clashes between reason and emotions such as shame or anger, or clashes between these emotions and urges for merely bodily or sensory gratification. His postulate of distinct calculative, appetitive, and spirited parts, sometimes simplified to a binary division between rational and nonrational impulses, not only takes account of psychological conflict but also registers the advantages of careful reflection over passion.

Plato actually appealed to Homer, to justify his proposal that the soul contains both rational and nonrational parts. The Homeric line that Plato cites runs as follows (*Odyssey* 20.17):

> Odysseus struck his chest, and rebuked his heart *(kradie)*.[11]

Plato comments (*Republic* 4.441b):

> Homer clearly portrays two different elements. The part that has reasoned about what is better and what is worse rebukes the part that is irrationally angry.

Was Plato right to find Homer anticipating his own theory of a complex soul in Homer and to attribute "reasoning" *(analogisamenon)* to Odysseus?

Odysseus has just observed the lascivious maids, who, in his absence from Ithaca, have been consorting with the suitors of Penelope. I translate *Odyssey* 20.9–14:

> Odysseus's spirit *(thumos)* rose up within his chest. He deliberated greatly within his

lungs *(phren)* and his spirit—whether he should rush out and slay each woman, or let them sleep for one last time with the arrogant suitors? At these thoughts his heart *(kradie)* within was barking like a bitch as she takes her stand around her helpless puppies.... Just so his heart barked as he fumed at the bad deeds.

Now comes the line already quoted: "Odysseus struck his chest, and rebuked his heart." This passage shows that Homer has all the resources he needs to express mental conflict and internal debate, meaning a strong impulse to act impulsively or passionately, while simultaneously or consecutively thinking better of it. Homer employs three words, *thumos, phren,* and *kradie* (compare the English expression "with heart *and* soul"), to characterize the strength of Odysseus's angry impulse, treating it as a force within the hero's body. He does not say, as Plato very likely would have done, that it was Odysseus's mind or reason that checked his passion. That checking, in the Homeric context, is done by Odysseus himself (the whole man), as he addresses one of the psychosomatic terms: "Bear up, my heart, you have endured worse than this."

Plato read these lines as confirmation of his theory that the human *psyche* is composed of distinct parts, one of them generating and signifying anger and the other one reason and reflection. That would be a plausible interpretation of Homer if the poet had distinguished rational and nonrational parts of a single psychological entity engaged in competition for the person's final decision and action. Plato's reading is instructive, but not fully accurate. What Homer does is actually something more interesting but quite experientially plausible, perhaps even more plausible than Plato's simultaneously divided self. Homer uses three of his psychosomatic terms (*thumos, phren,* and *kradie*) to identify the phases of Odysseus's passion and inner turmoil and to register his difficulty in containing them. He then concludes with the words of Odysseus, rebuking his heart, which is, of course, an essential part of himself, and thus tantamount to Odysseus's telling *himself,* "Hey, bear up." Rather than depict mental conflict as a battle between rational and nonrational parts of a Platonic soul, Homer uses his psychosomatic terms to signify an emotional activity within Odysseus's body, which Odysseus, the complete man, can address and resist. The psychosomatic terms signify angry and impulsive feelings, such as we all recognize and confront. The rational or intelligent opposition is voiced by Odysseus in response to these feelings. Odysseus and his feelings are not numerically distinct entities. They are distinguished or distinguishable just to the extent necessary to mark the reflexive nature of self-conscious experience.

Odysseus, of course, is an exceptional character in Homer. Most of Homer's figures, divine as well as human, are largely or entirely driven by their emotions. They do not display the prudence that enables Odysseus to control his feelings (that is to say, himself) in order to pursue his ultimate goals. Although Homer does not attribute reason as such to Odysseus, the wily character of the hero, along with his capacity to survive against great odds, strongly influenced the Greek philosophers in their focus on the blessings of rationality.

Homer's simile of the howling dog, as an image for Odysseus's passion, also left a strong impression on Plato. The ideal soldiers in his *Republic* are characterized by the dominance of *thumos* in their souls, a quality that supposedly makes them loyal to their friends and fierce to their enemies.[12] Plato's ideal rulers, on the other hand, are philosophers. They are characterized by souls whose *thumos* is subordinate to what Plato calls the rational element *(logistikon)*.

Here we do arrive at a concept that is at most implicit in Homer and pre-Platonic literature in general.

Reason or rationality *(logos)* is the faculty of mature human nature that Plato took to be fundamental to living and understanding a good life. The topic is so complex yet so central to later chapters of this book that I will explain it here only to the extent necessary to complete what I want to say about Homer's psychological models. According to Plato, reason equips human beings with two great capacities—the capacity for self-rule and the capacity for abstract and theoretical reflection. For convenience, we may call the first capacity ethical, and the second cognitive. The ethical capacity is based on the presupposition that our souls, in order to function well, must be organized on the model of a well-governed society. The cognitive capacity rests on the presumption that the soul, in its rational capacity, can discern ultimate truths by means of pure reasoning.

Homer knows nothing of political organization in the way that would be required for him to postulate analogous psychological metaphors of ruler and ruled, divide the person into a rightful governor and a subordinate populace, and apply these notions to one's mental and moral makeup. He does not represent a *thumos* as being well or badly governed (though

PSYCHOSOMATIC IDENTITY

he may call it "manly" or "noble" or "piteous"). Plato's ethical capacity requires that the soul be divided into distinct parts in order that the best part (reason) may rule over the worst part (sensual appetite) and ensure that our basic appetites and impulses are controlled accordingly. As for cognitive capacity, that was hardly available for anyone to clearly articulate before the development of mathematics and cosmology.

Homer's psychology lacks these distinctively Platonic capacities. This does not mean, of course, that Homeric characters cannot reason. Homer has great resources to distinguish farsighted and admirable actions from rash and wrongful behavior. Penelope acts prudently, in accordance with her regular epithet *pepnumenos,* and the story of Odysseus, as I have remarked, befits his recurrent epithets "much-enduring" and "wily." Achilles, Homer's psychologically most interesting character, can even engage in counterfactual reasoning, and wish that the world were different from what he finds it to be.[13] But, to the extent that Homer has a concept of soul that we can compare with Plato's, it is not a concept of psychologically distinct capacities or parts, or a subject for praise or blame, or a human capacity that could be trained or improved. Homer's agents are not souls. They are complete, embodied persons—much-enduring

Odysseus, wise Penelope, and fleet-footed Achilles. They are not composites of souls and bodies.

Like Plotinus, with whom I began this chapter, Plato has a dualistic conception of human beings as incorporeal souls inhabiting mortal bodies. The Platonic dialogues even contain arguments designed to prove that people's souls existed as intelligent entities before birth and will continue to exist as full-fledged persons after death. We may wonder whether Plato himself regarded any of these arguments as fully cogent, but we can be certain that he regarded the soul, and the essence of human nature and identity, as something nonphysical or spiritual, rather than material and essentially embodied. Whether we find the Platonic soul more convincing than Homer's psychosomatic conception of human identity, or judge it a piece of pious mythology, will depend on our preconceptions and intuitions rather than empirical facts. Platonism and Christianity have shaped language and thought in directions that are very different from Homer's vibrant representation of the union of mind and body. My aim in this chapter has been to present the Homeric model in its own terms as an effective account of experience, both from our first-person perspectives and from the way we observe other people. I don't wish to judge it superior or inferior to Plato's models of mind, but rather to indicate both how it strongly differs from Platonism and how it anticipates some of Plato's ideas.

Philosophical psychology, or what is sometimes called moral psychology, is not science. Modern psychology, working with experiments and statistics, seeks to establish value-free models of human behavior, with the aim of telling us the empirical facts. The ancient philosophers could analyze thoughts and feelings with great insight and behavioral accuracy, but their investigations were always tinged with an interest in norms—that is, ideas about what a mind could and should be like at its best. Ancient models of mind and self were also shaped by the literary and social contexts of their authors. Homer, aiming to delight his listeners with tales of epic grandeur, describes thought and action with incomparable immediacy. This literary genius enables us to know in our hearts what his characters feel in theirs, and that, by itself, is enough to tell us that Homer was a sophisticated psychologist.

Postscript on the Concept of Mind

Do human beings "have" minds or souls in the same sense that we say that we "have" arms or legs or hearts or brains? Some philosophers have thought so. Descartes in particular believed that the mind is a special kind of substance, a non-bodily substance within the body. Plato and Plotinus believed something rather similar about the *psyche*. If we think that these philosophers were right, we will be tempted, like Bruno Snell (in *The Discovery of the Mind*), to find fault with Homer for his lack of such a notion. But if we agree with such modern philosophers as Gilbert Ryle (in *The Concept of Mind*) that the Cartesian theory of mind is a myth (Ryle tartly called it the "ghost in the machine," followed by Clarke 1999 excerpted above), we may find Homer's lack of such dualism something greatly to be welcomed. According to Ryle, there is no such *thing* as the mind. Rather, the concept of mind, properly understood, identifies the category of human behavior involved in respect to thinking, feeling, and acting. Mind, according to Ryle, is the dispositional faculty that we exercise when we talk or calculate or choose and so forth. The word *mind* does not identify some special kind of spiritual entity inside our physical frame, and minds cannot exist independently from that physical frame.

This is not the place to elaborate or defend Ryle's account of the mind. I mention it here because readers of this book will find it an illuminating perspective from which to view the range of Greek ideas on the subject.

Further Reading

Clarke, M. (1999), *Flesh and Spirit in the Songs of Homer: A Study of Words and Myths* (Oxford).

Claus, D. B. (1981), *Toward the Soul: An Inquiry into the Meaning of Psyche before Plato* (New Haven).

Gill, C. (1996), *Personality in Greek Epic, Tragedy, and Philosophy: The Self in Dialogue* (Oxford).

Long, A. A. (2007), "Williams on Greek Literature and Philosophy," in A. Thomas, ed., *Bernard Williams* (Cambridge, UK), 155–80.

Pelliccia, H. (1995), *Mind, Body, and Speech in Homer and Pindar* (Göttingen).

Redfield, J. M. (1975), *Nature and Culture in the Iliad: The Tragedy of Hector* (Chicago).

Remes, P. (2008), *Neoplatonism* (Berkeley/Los Angeles).

Rohde, E. (1925), *Psyche: The Cult of Souls and the Belief in Immortality among the Greeks*; translation of *Psyche: Seelencult und Unsterblichkeitsglaube der Griechen* by W.B. Hillis (London; first published in German in 1893).

Ryle, G. (1949), *The Concept of Mind* (London).

Snell, B. (1953), *The Discovery of the Mind: The Greek Origins of European Thought*; translation of *Die Entdeckung des*

Geistes, 2nd ed. (Göttingen, 1948) by T. G. Rosenmeyer (Oxford).

Wilkes, K. (1988), *Real People: Personal Identity without Thought Experiments* (Oxford), especially chapter 7, "Models of Mind."

Williams, B. (2008) *Shame and Necessity*, 2nd ed. (Berkeley/Los Angeles).

2

INTIMATIONS OF IMMORTALITY

THE FOCUS OF Chapter 1 was the psychosomatic model of human identity that we find in the epic poetry of Homer. According to this model, living human beings are *essentially* embodied. All that remains of persons once they have breathed their last is a ghostly replica of the previously embodied person, a mere phantom or lifeless shade. Homer has no conception of an immortal soul such as we find in Plato and the Platonic tradition. In contrast with the immortal gods *(athanatoi),* Homer's human beings are *brotoi.* This Greek word is etymologically related to the English word *mortal.* While the Olympian gods feed on ambrosia and nectar, human beings are "bread eaters." They are doomed to die and to fall short of the gods in many other ways. Whether by beauty, knowledge, strength, or happiness, the Homeric gods are ideals that human beings can at best emulate and approximate. "Likeness to a god" is the highest praise a human being can obtain in Homer's epic world.

This gap between the immortal gods and mortal human beings provides Homeric poetry with much of its emotive greatness. Gods live "easy lives." They can turn their backs on the human world whenever they feel like it, to feast and play on Olympus. Unlike toiling humans, the gods risk nothing, or at least nothing that can affect their immortal status and special divine powers. The *Iliad* repeatedly emphasizes the finality of death. This finality has enormous pathos because Homeric warriors are obsessed with their renown and with what will be said about them after they are dead. "Undying fame" is the driving ambition of the Homeric warrior—the hope and goal that his name and his deeds will forever live on the lips of future generations. The imperishability of fame is the spur to courage, to the extent that Achilles, the greatest hero, has chosen a short and glorious life instead of a longevity that will not be remembered. But imperishable fame, far from mitigating the pathos of Homeric death, underlines death's finality. Death signifies the fact that those who will be immortalized in epic saga have actually ended their lives once and for all.

INTIMATIONS OF IMMORTALITY

This finality is often signified in Homer by accounts of the departure of the *psyche* from the body. Here are some instances: A warrior's "*psyche* left him, and night poured over his eyes"; "the *psyche* fled from the limbs and descended to Hades"; "a man's *psyche* cannot be restored once it has left the barrier of the teeth." When Odysseus encounters his mother's shade in the underworld, she explains the conditions of mortality to him (*Odyssey* 11.215–22):

> Our sinews no longer grip our flesh and bones,
> but they are destroyed by the fierce fire as soon
> as the *thumos* [life breath] departs from our
> white bones, and the *psyche* flies away like a
> dream.

The Homeric *psyche* never reenters the dead body that the life breath previously animated, though it may return to a person who has merely fainted. What the *psyche* may do, after death, is revisit the living, but it can do so only as a ghost. This apparition occurs in the *Iliad* (23.65–107) when the *psyche* of the dead Patroclus appears to Achilles in a dream and addresses him with requests to be awarded funeral honors. Patroclus, because he has not yet been buried, is unable to gain admittance to Hades. Achilles attempts to embrace the shade, "but it vanished like a wisp of smoke, and went gibbering underground." Achilles responds to this ghostly experience by remarking that deceased human beings are survived by a *psyche* and a wraith *(eidolon)*, but he also states that this ghostly replica is mindless (in Greek, without *phrenes*).

As living mortals, human beings in Homer are marked by a great range of moral and mental qualities—bravery and cowardice, wisdom and stupidity, honorableness and treachery, generosity and meanness. But as shades, these human beings have ceased to be living persons. Death levels all without distinction. There are neither rewards for the good to experience nor punishments for the bad to suffer. All shades are mindless and insubstantial. Or, at least that is how they present themselves to Odysseus until he miraculously revives them with sacrificial drinks of blood, enabling them to communicate with him, though not with one another.

If we proceed to Plato directly after reading Homer, we will be struck by the very different destiny and eschatology that Plato presents in the myths he includes in some of his greatest dialogues.[1] In these stories the postmortem *psyche* is no senseless ghost. It is the bodiless but mentally and morally complete survivor of the previously embodied person. Platonic *psychai,* on leaving the body in death, retain their minds and moral character without needing to be revived by blood. While Homeric *psychai,* on permanently leaving their bodies, are merely ex-persons, Platonic *psychai,* according to these myths, continue to be real; they are subject to postmortem judgment, rebirth, punishment, or reward. It is these *psychai* and not the bodies they have left behind that contain essential human identity. In Plato, by contrast with Homer, human identity is not psychosomatic but essentially "psychic," meaning that it is mental and moral, rather than vibrantly physical.

As I remarked in my Introduction and in Chapter 1, these contrasting models of human identity demand explanation. The principal difference between Homer and Plato is not, as has often been stated, the absence from Homer of any idea of a soul or of a mental and emotional center for the living person. As I argued before, Homer has the words for, and the conceptions of, what we call mind or soul or spirit in modern languages. The most salient difference between Homer and Plato is the one I just mentioned—the difference between taking the disembodied soul or spirit to be only a ghostly replica of the living person, and the Platonic conception that the soul outlives the body because it, and not the body, is the true seat of the person not only in embodied life, but even before birth and after death.

Christianity and other religions have familiarized us with something like the Platonic conception, at least in the sense that individual human spirits may be thought to have a life that continues beyond their mortal bodies. That familiarity may make the Homeric notion of death's absolute finality surprising or disappointing. Yet, setting faith and spiritualism aside, Homer's psychosomatic notion of human identity is empirically persuasive. What reasons could we have, other than wish fulfillment, for thinking that our life continues *for us* after the body has irrevocably ceased to breathe or move, and grows cold? (I emphasize *for us* in order to make room for the Homeric acknowledgment that human beings can have a surrogate afterlife if they continue to be remembered as heroes after death.) To approach the huge question of reasons for belief in a personally continuing afterlife, I return briefly to my initial contrast between divine immortality and excellence, and human mortality and limitation.

The Homeric gods are superior to human beings in the many ways that I already mentioned, but they are not superior morally. Just like human beings, they often act angrily or cruelly or unfairly; they lie and they deceive. Their superiority, in other words, transcends morality. This feature earned the Homeric gods Friedrich Nietzsche's approval because of his virulent contempt for Christian piety and sacrifice. Zeus, the principal Greek god, is a partial exception to this moral indifference. Zeus underwrites such moral principles as good treatment of strangers, the obligation of keeping oaths, and respect for suppliants, but his role in these respects is not central to the epic action; even Zeus, like the gods in general, is only intermittently interested in human beings. The gods, or at least most of them, may disapprove of a human action, as when Achilles disgraces the corpse of Hector by dragging it around the walls of Troy with his chariot. But for the most part, at least in the *Iliad,* human success or failure has little to do with a person's merits or character. Hector, fighting to defend his home and country, does not deserve to be killed by Achilles. Judged by moral criteria, Hector is much the better man. But Achilles, with a divine mother, has the higher pedigree, and he is the stronger man. This realistic emphasis on power, rather than justice, persists in the *Odyssey*. But in this,

GREEK MODELS OF MIND AND SELF

certainly the later, poem we are also given a strong sense that Odysseus deserves to recover his homeland and that the suitors who have supplanted him in his absence deserve their punishment at his hand.

What neither epic proposes with any assurance is that good or bad conduct will actually result in divine favor or the reverse. Human success or failure in Homer has much more to do with chance or divine partiality than with merit or a clear conception of justice. Menelaus, hardly the greatest hero, will go to Elysium, the Homeric equivalent of everlasting bliss, when he dies, although he has done nothing to deserve this exceptional destiny. It is accorded to Menelaus because, as the husband of Helen, he is related to Zeus by marriage. We can be fairly sure that Elysium, like the eternal punishments meted out to Tantalus and other great sinners in Hades, is an idea extraneous to the main oral traditions that have given rise to Homeric epic.

Hesiod, who composed his poems at much the same time that the Homeric epics were recorded, reflects some very different ideas about life and death, and about the connections between merit and prosperity. These notions have much in common with Near Eastern tales such as we find in the Sumerian epic of

INTIMATIONS OF IMMORTALITY

Gilgamesh and the Hebrew Bible. Unlike Homer's sagas, with heroes living close to the Olympian gods, Hesiod's two main themes are the daily life of a peasant farmer and the divine origin and organization of the world. Because of Homer's poetic splendor, scholars have tended to underestimate Hesiod's significance in the genealogy of Greek ideas about human identity and selfhood. Hesiod has no great figures like Odysseus and Penelope. His narratives take little interest in the psychology of human beings. He tells us nothing about the *psyche* of individual persons whether in life or after death. In the one place where he uses the word (*Works and Days* 686) it signifies the "life" that "pitiful mortals" risk when they go to sea for trade. For these reasons Hesiod may appear to be irrelevant to this book.

That assessment would be mistaken. Hesiod has one character with a highly elaborated psychology, namely Zeus, the principal divinity of the Greek pantheon. As an immortal, Zeus does not have a *psyche*, but like the Olympian gods in Homer, Hesiod's Zeus is fully equipped with all the faculties that explain human thoughts and feelings. Hesiod dwells upon the divine mind in his account of how the Titan Prometheus attempted to deceive Zeus (*Theogony* 507–616). There we are told of Zeus's anger (*thumos*) and of the impossibility for anyone to trip up his intellect (*noos*). The intellect of Zeus is an equally strong theme in Hesiod's *Works and Days* (105, 483, 661).

Hesiod is also of great significance for "intimations of immortality," this chapter's title. To explain why, I turn to four of Hesiod's great themes: the Golden Age and its aftermath, the myth of Prometheus, the justice of Zeus, and the punishment for divine oath breakers.

Homer's world is an epoch without any strong historical or evolutionary aspects. Hesiod's poems, by contrast, are permeated by notions of the past and of how the future will be shaped by people's previous and present actions. This temporal dimension is most clearly marked by Hesiod's saga of the five successive ages of man—golden, silver, bronze, heroic, and iron (*Works and Days* 109–210). Omitting the heroic age for now, the sequence from golden to iron represents a degeneration from the best to the worst, from an age of innocence to an age of crime. The Golden Age takes us back to the primeval era of Cronus, the father of Zeus.

Hesiod tells that, first of all, the immortal Olympian gods made a golden race of human beings. These people lived easy and trouble-free lives, "like gods." Their deaths were gentle. After death, we are told,

INTIMATIONS OF IMMORTALITY

"they became divine spirits *(daimons)*, guardians of mortal human beings and givers of wealth."[2] Was this "spiritual" destiny something the Golden Age people merited? Hesiod does not say so, but our text connects their postmortem, guardian role with keeping watch on court judgments and wicked deeds. We seem, then, to have the idea of an original human race (or rather an original race of males) that was not only granted an uninterruptedly happy life but was also morally good or at least innocent, and therefore suitable, after death, to play a watchful role for future human society. With this golden race, who survive death as divine spirits, Hesiod departs strikingly from Homeric anthropology and eschatology, with its emphasis on the absolute finality of death.

Hesiod alludes specifically to Homeric epic with his fourth race of heroes, who include those "who went to Troy for the sake of Helen." Intriguingly, Hesiod continues by saying that "while death's finality covered some of them there," Zeus sent others to the Isles of the Blessed, where they continue to enjoy the trouble-free life that the golden people had lived in the first of this sequence of five ages. In Homer, as we saw, Menelaus has been vouchsafed a very special afterlife, but in Hesiod this privilege is extended to other nameless heroes as well. We should notice, too, that Hesiod says nothing about why these privileged heroes had the blessing of transference to Elysium rather than a ghostly existence in the gloom of Hades. Hesiod himself, however, living in the grim Age of Iron, does not mention the prospect of any afterlife for himself or his fellow countrymen, whether a time of bliss or the reverse.[3]

What Hesiod does envision, again in striking contrast to Homer, is that the gods reward just conduct by making one's present life prosper. The farmer who keeps his oaths, works hard, and does not cheat will flourish: "Neither famine nor disaster ever haunts men who do true justice ... they flourish continually with good things" (ibid., 230–36). The life of the just person is comparable to the life of the Golden Age men, but with the difference that just persons have to work for their living in order to fully and explicitly deserve their prosperity. As for wrongdoers, Hesiod issues severe warnings. "Often even a whole city suffers for a bad man" (ibid., 239), with the people having to endure famine and plague. If the wrongdoer himself escapes disaster, retribution will eventually be visited upon his descendants. It is as though divine punishment for wrongdoing, if it does not immediately affect the perpetrator, will be transmitted to offspring through the wrongdoer's genes.

INTIMATIONS OF IMMORTALITY

According to Hesiod, Justice *(Dike)* is a goddess, no less a one than a daughter of Zeus. She has the special role of reporting human wrongdoing to her father, with a view to giving him the information he may use in order to punish wrongdoers or reward the innocent. Hesiod's manner of discourse is mythical, but it is not difficult to see that this notion of divinely watchful Justice imports a strong moral dimension into how he construes the basic fabric of the universe. Hesiod underscores this moral fabric by drawing the following distinction between human beings and all other creatures, a distinction ordained by none other than Zeus. The way of life (Hesiod's word is *nomos*) granted to the animals is "to eat one another" (ibid., 276–8). To human beings, by contrast, the way of life is justice *(dike)*.

From the poem of Gilgamesh, the biblical book of Genesis, and other Near Eastern material, we can infer that the ancestors of the Greeks were familiar with various myths concerning human origins. These myths will have included the idea of a lost paradise, of primordial wrongdoing, of divine retribution, of mortality, and of at least partial recovery of divine approval. Optimism and pessimism alternate in these sagas. The book of Genesis begins by celebrating the excellence of God's creation of the human race. But, immediately thereafter, Adam and Eve forfeit immortality and paradise by disobediently seeking to achieve the knowledge that will put them on the same level as God himself. Hesiod, like the author of Genesis, offers the optimism of the Golden Age and the pessimism of the Age of Iron. Just as the Genesis story insists on obedience to God as the way for human beings after Eden to flourish, so Hesiod tells the corrupt princes he is addressing to stick to justice.

Were the original human beings divine, and are human beings in the present fallen gods? These are questions that Hesiod and his contemporaries hardly posed in these explicit terms. I ask them here because I believe that affirmative answers to them underlie much of the thinking that gave rise to beliefs in an immortal soul whose destiny, whether good or bad, has been irrevocably shaped by a person's moral conduct. This, of course, is the eschatology familiar to us from Plato's myths. Plato credits the human soul with a divine origin, and supposes it to have had extraordinary cognitive experience before becoming embodied and then forgetting what it has previously known.

Hesiod does not say anything like that. However, according to the most plausible interpretation of his

INTIMATIONS OF IMMORTALITY

Prometheus myth, Hesiod envisioned a phase in the world's development when men (I mean males) and gods had lived together (*Theogony* 535–616). That phase came to an end during a feast that all had shared. Prometheus attempted to trick Zeus by giving men the better portions of an ox that he had cut up. Zeus reacted by withholding fire from men's society. Prometheus stole it back for them, and Zeus created woman as punishment. The details and logic of this remarkable story are quite obscure. What it serves, for my purpose here, is further illustration of Hesiod's notion that he himself was living in an era when human beings had lost their original happy communion with gods.

Shortly, I will turn to our first explicit allusions outside mythology to human prospects for immortality, and the recovery of divinity. Before that, however, there is a further story about the gods in Hesiod that merits close attention (*Theogony* 782–806). Any Olympian god who breaks an oath is compelled for an entire year to taste no nectar or ambrosia. The result is a death-like state, during which the god lies "breathless and speechless," just like a Homeric shade. This is not the end of the god's punishment. For a further nine years the foresworn god is banished from divine deliberations and feasts. The story is packed with a strong moral charge in the temporary reduction of the sinning god to a mortal condition, the notion that oath breaking is a crime of exceptional gravity, and the expulsion of a foresworn god from divine company. All these ideas are given a place in our earliest accounts of what happens after death to the souls of human wrongdoers.

As I turn now to this eschatological material, I ask my readers to keep in mind the points I have made, to illustrate Hesiod's difference from Homer's constant emphasis on human mortality, the corresponding distance of human beings from divinity, and the absence of anything in Homer that resembles Hesiod's stories about justice, crime, punishment, and reward. To be sure, the *Iliad* was set in motion by the wrong that Paris did to Menelaus by seducing and stealing Helen of Sparta, when he was a guest in Menelaus's house. But in Homer there is nothing comparable to the following lines of Hesiod with their remarkable personifications (ibid., 217–21):

> Oath runs along with crooked judgments....
> Justice, in tears, haunts the city and the people
> who have expelled her and mistreated her.

INTIMATIONS OF IMMORTALITY

Homeric epic has great resources to make moral judgments, but it never personifies justice, and it does not construe human identity in fundamentally moral terms. Hesiod's poetry, by contrast, is packed with tales of crime and punishment, and it emphasizes the blessings of good conduct. Hesiod does not enter into the minds of his characters, but the themes I have highlighted anticipate much of the moral psychology that Plato will elaborate in great depth.

If human identity is fundamentally moral, and if human beings owe their life to their soul, then their soul too must be fundamentally marked by its moral judgments and moral character. If that is so, justice seems to require that a good soul should fare better than a bad one. Yet, experience of everyday life does not offer strong support to such outcomes, at least if faring well is construed in such Hesiodic ways as a farmer's fertile fields and livestock, and flourishing families.

One way to connect goodness of soul with faring well is to detach prosperity from material benefit altogether and construe human flourishing largely or entirely in terms of virtuous character. This was the route that Socrates took (Plato, *Apology* 29d) when he proclaimed at his trial in Athens that goodness of soul should be valued far ahead of any bodily and external benefits like one's social status and reputation. If that Socratic proposition is sound, we may infer that goodness of soul is desirable for its own sake, or at least largely irrespective of its consequences. If, on the other hand, we think that justice should be rewarded partially, if not entirely, in more conventionally desirable ways, we might hope that a good but unfortunate life in this world will be counterbalanced by a prosperous postmortem destiny, like transference to the Isles of the Blessed. In that case, the just but unfortunate person will need to have a soul that provides a continuing existence after death. And so we come at length to the remarkable idea of an immortal soul that continues the life of the previously embodied person.

Our earliest accounts of this belief in ancient Greece date from about 500 BCE. At around that time Pythagoras founded a cult whose ritual practices were believed to purify his followers and help them achieve a good afterlife. Pythagoras and his followers were vegetarians. Their abstinence from eating meat was connected with the belief that the human soul, after leaving its present body, may migrate into the bodies of other kinds of animals, with the type of animal fitting the character that the human being had had in his earlier incarnation. At around the same time, cults associated with the god Dionysus and with the death of the mythical poet Orpheus began to proliferate. These cults too promised their adherents a superior afterlife in return for appropriate conduct during their present existence.[4]

The evidence about Pythagoras and Orphism is very difficult to interpret. The one thing about it that I need to stress here is that at the date I have indicated, some two hundred years after Homer and Hesiod, beliefs concerning a genuine afterlife had begun to circulate—not beliefs about the merely ghostly survival of the human *psyche* but about its continuation as the core of a living person with the quality of its afterlife dependent on the moral quality of its previously embodied life. Some of these beliefs involved *metempsychosis,* the idea that the human soul may migrate into different types of living creature; other beliefs did not include this doctrine. What matters for my present purpose is not transmigration of the soul as such, intriguing though that idea is, but the sheer boldness of the notion that human beings continue to have a real life after their present body has ceased to exist. If that is right, the essence of human identity is no longer psychosomatic, as we found it to be in Homer, but psychic. I shall focus attention on two authors who transmit such views—Pindar and Empedocles.

Pindar was the author of lyric poems celebrating victories in one of the Greeks' annual athletic competitions. He consistently reflects the aristocratic values of his patrons, who have hired him to praise their competitive prowess and the glories of their lineage. His odes, to be sung and danced by choruses, embellish the fame and achievement of victors together with the wealth and honor that victory confers on their families. Pindar interweaves historical fact with myth and religion. In this way he creates a lyrical panorama that combines eulogy with typically Greek warnings against the human excesses and ambition that can bring divine resentment. For the most part Pindar's ideas about the good life are entirely traditional. He typically contrasts human mortality with divine immortality, the great Homeric theme that I emphasized at the beginning of this chapter. When he refers to *psyche,* generally either he signifies the cognitive and emotional center of living persons, exactly in the way that Homer signifies these things with the words *thumos* or *phrenes,* or he alludes to the shade that leaves the body at death and then passes irrevocably to Hades. There is nothing novel

INTIMATIONS OF IMMORTALITY

about Pindar's treatment of identity and selfhood, at least for the most part.

In a few passages, however, Pindar makes cryptic reference to a quite different belief system.[5] He writes of *psychai* that are *returned* to life on earth after spending time in Hades. From these souls, he says, develop noble kings and mighty men, renowned for their strength and wisdom—men who hereafter are called holy heroes. The surrounding context of these remarks hardly explains what exactly Pindar has in mind, but there can be no doubt that he postulates rebirth for certain human beings. He does not say, in so many words, that these persons' souls are immortal, but we must at least infer that the souls from which the noble kings and mighty men develop were already embodied in an earlier life, and that they went on to earn a further resplendent life in the underworld. In a further text, again without a surrounding context, Pindar tells of a glorious subterranean world that is illuminated by its own sun. The inhabitants of this world enjoy games and music and every other delight, calling to mind Hesiod's Golden Age.

Pindar has more to say about this kind of eschatology in his second *Olympian Ode*. He wrote this poem to honor the chariot race victories of Theron, ruler of the splendid Syracusan city of Acragas (modern Agrigento). Pindar begins by praising Theron for his virtues. He then traces the ups and downs, or rather, the downs and ups, of Theron's family line. We learn that Theron's ancestors reached their lowest point with Oedipus and his fratricidal sons. However, subsequent generations, thanks to their prowess, have restored Theron's family distinction. Pindar then draws a moral from these genealogical vicissitudes. Wealth, he says, creates great opportunities, but prosperity will not follow in the long term unless those who have wealth behave justly. This of course is the dominant message of Hesiod that I have already discussed. To ensure that we note the allusion to Hesiod, Pindar tells us that morally observant people, exemplified by those who keep their oaths, enjoy an idyllic life, whereas wrongdoers have a very bad time.

This sounds quite traditional, and so it is in Pindar's representation of the delights that the good enjoy. But Pindar, unlike Hesiod, also associates these woes and delights with the new eschatology I summarized a moment ago. Now I translate:

> All who have endured to keep their soul *(psyche)*
> completely free from wrongdoing, three times
> on either side, travel the road of Zeus to the

INTIMATIONS OF IMMORTALITY

> citadel of Cronus. There on the island of the
> blessed... golden flowers shine forth, and
> those dwelling there experience paradise.

Cadmus, the distant ancestor of Theron, is present in this Elysium. He has presumably earned his place. Pindar also observes that Achilles is there (not in Hades, as he is in Homer's account of the dead). In this case, no merit was at work, however. Achilles enjoys a blissful afterlife because his mother Thetis persuaded Zeus with her prayers.

With the mention of keeping one's soul free from wrongdoing, Pindar seems to have forged a striking connection with rewards that the morally good have deserved because of their goodness, whereas malefactors endure postmortem punishment in the underworld. We did not find any trace of such postmortem rewards or punishments in Hesiod. But if Achilles can get to heaven, like Menelaus in Homer, merely thanks to divine favor, has Pindar produced a coherent moral story? The answer is that he has not. Apart from the incoherence of combining merited and unmerited bliss in these ideas of what happens to people after death, Pindar is quite obscure in many details. We are given no clear idea of what he means by his reference to those who have kept their *psyche* "free from wrongdoing, three times, on either side." Does this succession mean an alternation of three pairs of good lives, each pair consisting of an earthly life followed by a life in Hades? This is the commonest interpretation, but if it is correct, how are we to understand *psyche*? Does the word mean "soul" in the way that Plato speaks of soul as distinct from body, or should we translate it simply as "life" or "self"? Pindar must be thinking of something much more substantial than the ghostly Homeric shade. As we already saw, he was aware of the idea that human beings are not restricted to living just one life. Most significantly, he combines that idea with the notion that the quality of future existence is conditioned by the quality of previous lives.

We can now understand why *psyche* became the standard Greek word for the soul or mind or self rather than the word *thumos,* which can often in Homer be rendered by mind or self. Both words are etymologically connected with breath, as we have seen from the fact that their permanent departure from the body signifies irrevocable loss of breath, and therefore death. However, *thumos* had been conceived as a part of the living person rather than the entire person as such. *Psyche,* by contrast, had already signified the whole of a person's life, as when

INTIMATIONS OF IMMORTALITY

Achilles is said to dispatch to Hades the *psychai* of many heroes, or to risk his own *psyche* on the battlefield without being adequately honored. Once the idea of an afterlife took hold, the original usage of *psyche* to mean an entire life made it the most appropriate word to also designate a person's postmortem existence. This may seem a remarkable extension from Homer's mindless ghosts, but on reflection it will be found quite intelligible in spite of scholarly claims to the contrary.

Has Pindar, then, given expression to a definite conception of the soul's immortality? Hardly. For that to be the case, we would need to know what he thought about the relationship between the continuing soul and the mortal bodies that it inhabits from time to time. Rather than addressing that question, Pindar has combined traditional ideas about Elysium with seemingly novel ideas about a morally characterized self that lives plural lives and is rewarded or punished accordingly. This idea is strikingly different from the Homeric finality of death. But Pindar shows no sign that he himself was aware of that momentous difference.

I don't know how to account for this curious combination of tradition and innovation. Here is a fascinating subject for further research. At least we can be sure that Pindar has not simply invented the idea that the same self can live plural lives. He almost certainly learned it in Sicily from Empedocles, who learned it in turn from the followers of Pythagoras, who were active at this time just across the sea in southern Italy. Pindar, as I mentioned, wrote his second *Olympian Ode* to honor the ruler of Acragas, the native city of the early Greek philosopher Empedocles. Pindar may have introduced ideas of rebirth and postmortem rewards and punishments primarily to please his Sicilian patron. If that was so, it should advise us that significant shifts in human consciousness and belief, or at least in our record of such things, may owe as much to chance as they do to deliberate intention or well-articulated imagination.

To introduce Empedocles, I quote this extraordinary passage from one of his philosophical poems:

> There is an oracle of Necessity, the gods'
> ancient and eternal decision, sealed by broad
> oaths. Whenever one of the divine spirits,
> assigned long life, pollutes its own limbs by
> sinful killing, and breaking of its oath, it is
> banished from the blessed ones for thirty
> thousand years. It is born into all kinds of

> mortal creatures, in a succession of harsh ways
> of life ... one element after another receives
> it [earth, air, fire, and water] and they all hate
> it. Of these spirits I too am one, a fugitive
> from the gods because I put my trust in insane
> strife.[6]

These remarkable words recall Hesiod's gods who are banished for a long period because of breaking their oaths. Empedocles also repeats the Pindaric idea of a succession of lives for the same individual, but he complicates that notion considerably. The lives into which Empedocles's sinful spirits are reborn are not only human, they also range across the entire spectrum of creatures. This destiny must reflect the influence of Pythagorean *metempsychosis*. In one of his verses Empedocles even includes himself as a banished spirit. He appears to be telling us that he and perhaps all other human beings have a genealogy that includes divinity. From other verses that he wrote, we can expand this extraordinary eschatology.

Empedocles looks back to a time of complete peace. This period preceded the Olympian gods and even the era of the more ancient Cronus. It was an epoch of paradise when divine Love alone ruled the universe. What brought this era to an end was the killing that polluted the spirits, in the sad passage quoted above. This killing was the beginning of blood sacrifice. Accordingly it ushered in the end of what had previously been an entirely vegetarian epoch. Human beings, we are told, had once regarded the killing of animals as the "greatest pollution." Now, as a result of such killing, they are doomed to a succession of lives in a sequence of different mortal forms in the way described. The world that had once been ruled by Love is now under the domain of Love's opposite, Strife. However, this is not the end of the banished spirits' fate, or at least not the end for some of them. Like Pindar, with his noble kings and heroes who develop from souls returned to earth from Hades, Empedocles envisions the final emergence of a special set of beings—prophets, physicians, and leaders—who will actually blossom into gods, and already include himself.

What are the implications of Empedocles's eschatology for our investigation of Greek ideas about the human self and identity? It may be helpful to spell them out as a series of postulates:

1. Human identity straddles numerous lifetimes and numerous life types.

2. The starting point of each human identity was a Golden Age of peace and innocence, when human beings were gods or godlike.
3. Human beings forfeited the Golden Age by failing to respect the lives of other creatures.
4. Some human beings can recover their divine or godlike status.

Questions that these postulates pose but do not answer include the following. Are the so-called spirits *(daimons)* what Pindar calls "souls" *(psychai)*? Do they have a bodily or visible form? In their original and recovered condition, do the spirits inhabit bodies that look like human beings?

Empedocles seems to have been interested in these questions, but we cannot precisely say how he envisioned the composition of the spirits. He intimates the long-term survival of something that appears to be a specifically human identity, but he does not actually call it a *psyche*. It has sufficiently "long life" to be named a divine spirit *(daimon)*, but that is hardly enough for us to say that it is immortal in the sense that it will live forever.[7] What chiefly marks the identity of Empedocles's banished spirits (like that of the exiles from Eden) is precisely the terrible fact of their banishment—the bliss that they have lost because of their murderous and carnivorous behavior. Their identity is based neither on their parentage nor on their social status nor on what they have done in any of their successive lives nor on their geographical location. The banished spirits are doomed to keep changing their species life. Empedocles even professes to tell those who read him that he himself has been a bird, a fish, and even a bush! That is a very discouraging succession of lives. Fortunately, it is not the final story, at least for him. He also proclaims to his fellow citizens that he goes about among them, as an immortal god, no longer mortal.

It is tempting to think that Empedocles must have been mad if he was fully serious in uttering such words. Let's leave that judgment on one side here. I prefer to read him not as giving us a crazy autobiography, but as adumbrating ideas about original sin and possibly ultimate redemption. In saying that, I don't in the least intend to make him a prefiguration of Augustine. My point is rather that Empedocles offers us intimations of immortality and an essentially moral basis to human identity. Like the hints of Pindar, these are a striking contrast to the psychosomatic self of Homeric epic.

"If one knows what is to come...." Pindar introduces his narrative about rebirth, rewards, and

INTIMATIONS OF IMMORTALITY

punishments with these solemn words. No one of course can ever truly *know* what happens to our embodied identity after death. But it is probably only human to hope that death is not the final end to the life we experience in our present embodied condition. We can certainly not imagine what it is like to be dead; for in that case, our imagination would run ahead and negate what it is supposed to be imagining. The bloodless and senseless shade of Homeric epic is as close as we are likely to come to picturing the dead remnant of a living self, whose identity continues to reside in the corpse that the shade has left. Just so, Homeric ghosts use personal pronouns about themselves. If they refer to their bodies, they say, "Please bury *me*."

A corpse is not a self. If there is such a thing as an immortal soul, it will have to forsake its present body in order to continue its existence. The ideas I have been exploring with the help of Hesiod, Pindar, and Empedocles will return with great force in Plato's dialogues. Rather than foreshadow those works, I end this chapter with a selection of thoughts proposed by Heraclitus, a philosopher who lived in the generation after Pythagoras but before Pindar and Empedocles. Heraclitus is especially apt to conclude this chapter because he makes hints and suggestions about the self and human nature, while leaving it to his audience to figure out the final answers.[8]

Heraclitus's deliberately enigmatic philosophy is typified in the following cryptic statement: "Mortal immortals; immortal mortals; living their death; dying their life." Homer had drawn a firm line between immortal gods and mortal human beings. Hesiod, Pindar, and Empedocles blur the distinction at times. Heraclitus offers a third perspective by saying, in his beautifully symmetrical statement, that death and life, mortality and immortality, far from excluding one another, are mutually implicated. If this is right, nothing is absolutely in one of these states or in the other: the dead are in some sense alive, and the living are in some sense dead. We would not expect that the author of such a riddle would enunciate a clear-cut doctrine concerning mortality and immortality, and indeed Heraclitus does not. Instead, he offers us such challenging and cryptic statements as the following:

> Unexpected and unimagined things await human beings when they die.
>
>   I searched for myself.
>
>   A human being's character *(ethos)* is his fate/ divine spirit *(daimon)*.

> You could not discover the limits of the soul *(psyche)* by going, even if you traversed every road; so deep is its measure *(logos)*.
>
> The soul's measure or reckoning *(logos)* is self-growing.[9]
>
> Souls that die in battle are purer than those that die from illness.
>
> Corpses are more deserving to be thrown out than dung.
>
> A dry soul is wisest and best.

Heraclitus is the only philosopher before Plato from whom we can recover an actual theory of the soul's nature and identity during our embodied life. He does not explicitly contrast the soul with the body, as Plato will do, but he clearly treats it as the essence of the living person. As Pindar would say, souls can vary in quality and purity, but Heraclitus was strikingly innovative in attributing the capacity for depth and something like autonomy ("self-growing") to the soul. The impossibility, as he puts it, of discovering the soul's limits may be read as a mark of our mind's extraordinary intellectual potentiality. Unlike Odysseus, who evoked the shades of the dead by journeying to the ends of the earth, Heraclitus proposes that self-understanding and psychology cannot be likened to a geographical quest. In order to discover who we are, we must learn to understand the evidence of our senses, inquire into the nature of things, overcome our separate personal attitudes, and seek to discover where we fit within the general structure of the world.

Heraclitus situated his deliberately riddling statements in a cosmology of radical flux whereby all things are constantly transformed in a regular and balanced cycle of changes—hot to cold, wet to dry, winter to summer, living to dead, and so forth. There is a measure (*logos*) that regulates this process, making it a rational system, which Heraclitus identified with what he calls "god." Conformity to the *logos* is Heraclitus's formula for an intelligent life, by keeping oneself in harmony with the rhythms of nature. He probably proposed, as Plato would propose in his dialogue *Phaedo,* that life and death have no final boundaries because souls are recycled in a succession that *we merely call* living and dying. Heraclitus treated fire as the world's primary element, motivated by the transformative and energizing powers of heat. Hence, we may understand why he says that hot and dry souls are the best for human beings, including the souls of those who die in the heat of battle. Whether Heraclitus envisioned an afterlife in which such souls, or perhaps all souls, are conscious of their previous existence, we cannot say. He may have wisely left that question open, leaving us to ponder his irrefutable statement that "unimagined and unexpected things happen to us when we die." This is not an explicit affirmation of immortality, but it definitely contests the finality and pathos of Homeric death.

Heraclitus was a philosopher in a recognizably modern sense. By this I mean that we can make use of his statements without having to presuppose the mythologies of Hesiod, Pindar, and Empedocles. Rather, with remarkable hints and suggestions about life and death, and about souls and corpses, Heraclitus challenges us to ask how we should make sense of our selves both as embodied animals and as beings with minds that can travel far beyond our bodily limits and limitations. In these ways Heraclitus originated the ideal of the contemplative life.

Further Reading

Adkins, A. (1960), *Merit and Responsibility: A Study in Greek Values* (Oxford).

Betegh G. (2004), *The Derveni Papyrus: Cosmology, Theology, and Interpretation* (Cambridge, UK).

Clarke, M. (1999), *Flesh and Spirit in the Songs of Homer: A Study of Words and Myths* (Oxford).

Dodds, E. R. (1951), *The Greeks and the Irrational* (Berkeley/Los Angeles).

Frede, D., and Reis, B. (2009), eds., *Body and Soul in Ancient Philosophy* (Berlin/New York).

Griffin, J. (1980), *Homer on Life and Death* (Oxford).

Guthrie, W. K. C. (1950), *The Greeks and Their Gods* (London).

Inwood, B. (1992), *The Poem of Empedocles: A Text and Translation with an Introduction* (Toronto).

Kahn, C. H. (1979), *The Art and Thought of Heraclitus: A New Arrangement and Translation of the Fragments with Literary and Philosophical Commentary* (Cambridge, UK).

—— (2001), *Pythagoras and the Pythagoreans: A Brief History* (Indianapolis).

Laks, A. (1999), "Soul, Sensation, and Thought," in Long, ed., *Cambridge Companion*, 250-70.

Lamberton, R. (1988), *Hesiod* (New Haven).

Lloyd-Jones, H. (1971), *The Justice of Zeus* (Berkeley/Los Angeles).

Long, A. A. (1999), ed., *The Cambridge Companion to Early Greek Philosophy* (Cambridge, UK).

—— (2009), "Heraclitus on Measure and the Explicit Emergence of Rationality," in Frede and Reis, eds., *Body and Soul*, 87-110.

McKirahan, R. (2010), *Philosophy before Socrates: An Introduction with Texts and Commentary,* 2nd ed. (Indianapolis).

Nietzsche, F. (1872), *The Birth of Tragedy;* translation of *Die Geburt der Tragödie aus dem Geiste der Musik* by W. Kaufmann (New York, 1974).

Partenie, C. (2009), ed., *Plato's Myths* (Cambridge, UK).

Snell, B. (1953), *The Discovery of the Mind: The Greek Origins of European Thought;* translation of *Die Entdeckung des Geistes* by T. G. Rosenmeyer (Oxford).

Vernant, J.-P. (1982), *Myth and Society in Ancient Greece* (London).

Walcot, P. (1966), *Hesiod and the Near East* (Cardiff).

3

BODIES, SOULS, AND
THE PERILS OF PERSUASION

TWO GREEK WORDS became the basis for the philosophers' ways of talking about human nature, the words that we translate into English as body *(soma)* and soul *(psyche)*. All ancient philosophers from Plato onward assume that theories about human nature should distinguish between the anatomical structure we call the body, and the mental, emotional, and ethical features that we call the mind or soul. This distinction was well established in Greek culture during Plato's lifetime. That is clear from the following remark by one of his contemporaries, the orator Isocrates:[1]

> It is generally agreed that our nature consists
> of both body and soul. No one would deny
> that, of these two, the soul is the more suited to

BODIES, SOULS, AND PERSUASION

> command and of greater value. For it is the function of the soul to deliberate about public and personal matters, and the function of the body to serve the soul's decisions.

Isocrates presumes that his readers will immediately understand his allocation of distinct values and functions to body and soul, and so we do, up to a point at least. If there is something noteworthy in what Isocrates says, from our modern perspective, this is probably his representing the functions of soul and body in a militaristic or political way. Isocrates likens these functions to the relation of a general to an army, or of a political leader to the populace at large, with the former taking command and the latter obediently serving.

This hierarchical relationship between body and soul was sometimes modeled on the subordination of slaves to masters. There are many examples of this metaphor in Plato and other writers of the time. A century later the Stoic philosophers drew on Isocrates's word "suited to command" *(hegemonikon)* as their name for the principal part of the soul, by which they meant the mind or intellect as distinct from our sensory faculties and metabolic functions. Western people have inherited this body/soul language in all kinds of ways that I need not exemplify here.

As I begin to make Plato the chief focus of this chapter and of Chapter 4, I want to emphasize the following point. Isocrates's distinction between the functions and values of body and soul may seem commonplace or obvious to us. In fact, however, it was far from being normal Greek practice a hundred years previously, at around the time when Socrates was born at Athens. The distinction is absent from Homer. As we saw in Chapter 1, the Homeric epics have the linguistic resources to express what we call the mind, as when in English we say what we think or feel or want, or when we refer to what is going on in our hearts or our heads. But Homeric expressions for the mind do not pick out something quite distinct in kind from a human being's physical features or anatomical organs. Apart from the absence of that distinction, Homer does not prioritize his expressions for mind in Isocrates's hierarchical manner of placing the soul in command of the body.

In Chapter 2 I showed when and how ideas concerning an afterlife for persons began to emerge in Greece. One way to describe postmortem existence was to endow the Homeric *psyche,* meaning life breath

BODIES, SOULS, AND PERSUASION

or vitality, with the capacity to go on living after the perishing of the body that the *psyche* had previously animated—not to continue as a mere ghost, as happens to the *psyche* in Homer, but to serve as the basis of a human identity that was no longer limited to a single perishable embodiment. However, such ideas in the material I presented were expressed in mythical terms. The authors who said such things did not explain how a person's identity or mind or self could continue outside and beyond the person's previous body. Moreover, the myths seemed to treat the continuing soul, if we call it that, as virtually a still embodied person, talking and moving around. These early afterlife myths do not invoke or imply a categorical distinction between body and soul or the physical and the mental.

It is true, of course, that Greek authors at the time of Socrates often used the words *soma* and *psyche*. But they did not generally use them in order to assign *soma* and *psyche* the functional and evaluative differences described by Isocrates in the statement quoted above. Greeks of the fifth century BCE could refer to either the living person or the corpse by the same term *soma*. They could use this word to signify a life, as when speaking about what one fights for, or what one serves, or what one deliberates about. They could use the word *psyche* similarly, or they could use *psyche* for the self or the character of a person. The figures represented in Greek drama can even describe *living* human beings as "mere shades" *(eidola),* or they may speak as if living human beings will have a full-scale afterlife in Hades, where they will be able to communicate with their deceased kindred. This fluidity of usage is not obscure or confusing, provided we do not expect that, for ordinary life, people who spoke in this way were trying to articulate theoretical notions of human nature. Today, too, we often use words like *body, person, self, human being, character,* and so forth quite interchangeably.

What was it, then, that prompted Greek thinkers to make sharp distinctions between body and soul in the way that I have exemplified from Isocrates? In Chapter 2 I proposed that notions of an independent existence for the soul were encouraged by the hopes of an afterlife, which would reward good conduct or make up for unjust treatment, and mitigate the finality of death. While I take that to be importantly true, the early authors or transmitters of such afterlife beliefs do not appear to have subscribed to Isocrates's hierarchical and functional distinction between body and soul. I will now argue that this distinction was

BODIES, SOULS, AND PERSUASION

particularly influenced by a special feature of Greek culture in the fifth century BCE, the strong development of rhetoric as an educational and political skill. The employment of rhetorical aptitude in political and judicial contexts helped to generate two big ideas about human psychology, first people's susceptibility to persuasive speech, and second the mentality people need to have in order to resist the power of rhetoric by the application of reason.

The key figures essential to establishing these points are Socrates (as characterized by Plato) and the celebrated Sicilian thinker Gorgias, who was born some ten years earlier.[2] Gorgias was renowned as a rhetorician and teacher of rhetoric, taking rhetoric to be the art of persuasion in large gatherings such as political assemblies and courts of law. Plato devoted one of his longest, weightiest, and probably earliest dialogues to drawing a stark and bitter contrast between the supporters of Gorgias, who are advocates of the per se value of political power and the freedom it supposedly confers, and a life devoted to justice and moderation, represented by Socrates.[3] To set the context for this encounter and its bearing on the theme of bodies and souls, we should start from the defense speech *(Apology)* that Plato assigned to

Socrates at his trial as a corrupter of the youth and a subverter of the Athenian state's religion.

Socrates begins the speech by disavowing his rhetorical ability, but the words Plato has assigned to him are actually a declamatory masterpiece. Although the *Apology* narrowly failed to persuade the members of the jury to acquit Socrates, it has convinced countless readers of the last twenty-four centuries that he was not only innocent of the charges brought against him but also a spokesman for uncompromising allegiance to rational inquiry, integrity, and beneficence. At the speech's climactic moments, Socrates imagines himself to be responding to someone who offers him acquittal on condition that he abandon his philosophical mission (29e–30b):

> Best of men, Athenian that you are, member of the city that is greatest and most renowned for wisdom and strength, are you not ashamed to care about maximizing your wealth and fame and status, but not to care or give thought for intelligence and truth and to making your soul as good as possible.... All I do is go about persuading you all, young and old, not to care for your bodies or your wealth with the zeal

> you should devote to making your soul as good as possible, by saying that it is not from wealth that goodness arises, but from goodness wealth and everything else become beneficial for human beings both in private and in public.

"Making your soul as good as possible"—that emphatically repeated phrase, according to Socrates, requires preferring intellectual and moral goods to the betterment of one's body and external circumstances.

Socrates in the *Apology* does not elaborate beyond this passage on the actual nature of the soul and the soul's difference from the body. At the end of the speech (40c–41c) he disclaims any fear of death, observing that either the dead are insentient nonentities or at death the *psyche* migrates to another place, where he might meet and converse with wonderful mythological persons. The two alternatives recall the Homeric witless shades on the one hand and, on the other hand, the blissful prospects that Pindar set forth for virtuous souls (see Chapter 2). Socrates's defense speech leaves the soul's final destiny unresolved.

Not so the *Gorgias*. In this confrontation with the partisans of rhetoric and the power it confers on its practitioners, Socrates maintains that persuasive discourse divorced from philosophy is no true skill, but simply a technique for pandering to an audience without regard to its harmful effects on their lives. Socrates starts this argument (464b–466a) by means of a schematic set of analogies. Rhetorical skill, he proposes, stands to the soul as the art of the pastry cook stands to the body. What genuinely regulates bodies is gymnastics, whereas cosmetics merely makes bodies look good. In the case of the soul the analog for gymnastics is legislation or justice, and the analog for cosmetics is sophistry or rhetoric. Without justice rhetoric is immensely harmful, according to Socrates. Moreover, the power it seems to give people is apparent only, not genuinely capable of giving those who use it the freedom to live as they really want to do.

The arguments that Socrates uses, to refute Gorgias and his defenders, depend heavily on distinctions between body and soul. Like Isocrates, Plato makes Socrates give the priority to soul over body, but the confrontation Plato stages between philosophy and rhetoric is developed in ways that go far beyond Isocrates's simple contrasts between a subordinate body and a commanding soul. Plato ends

BODIES, SOULS, AND PERSUASION

his dialogue with an extraordinary myth of the afterlife. Here souls are stripped of their former bodies, in order that they may be judged purely on the basis of their characters and their actions when they were alive. In this way the judges in Hades will know nothing about the social status or appearance that the souls had when they were previously embodied, and so they will judge them on purely moral grounds, uninfluenced by the appearance of things.

Plato's dualism of body and soul is one of the things best known about his philosophy. It is widely supposed that he learned it from Pythagorean thinkers when he visited Sicily. That may well be true. However, Gorgias himself (who was some fifty years older than Plato) must have known about Pythagoreanism. As a Sicilian, Gorgias must also have been familiar with the strange afterlife ideas of Empedocles that I discussed in Chapter 2. Empedocles had posited for each person a spirit *(daimon)* that passed from one kind of body to another kind of body in a long succession of lives. What I wish to do now, before returning to Plato's confrontation between Gorgias and Socrates, is to discuss a curiously neglected topic—the keen interest that Gorgias himself took in distinctions between soul and body. By Gorgias here, I mean texts written by the real man, not words put into his mouth as a character by Plato.

Further introductory words about Gorgias are in order because his philosophical work has been regularly undervalued. Gorgias is frequently presented as a mere sophist or even as a malign figure because of his pioneering role in the development of persuasive rhetorical techniques without apparent concern for the use made of them. In scholarly writings Plato has regularly overshadowed Gorgias. No reader of this book, I am sure, needs to be reminded of the social and political damage that irresponsible and hate-filled rhetoric has caused in modern history, and continues to cause as I write. Rather than judge Gorgias himself to have had a bad influence on Greek culture because rhetoric can be so easily misused, I take his impact to have been highly beneficial in certain ways. One way was his recognition that democratic politics and judicial procedure depend in part on rhetoric because persuasion through public discourse is their essential medium. In these spheres probability rather than demonstrated truth is typically at stake when the pro and contra of a policy are debated or the guilt or innocence of an accused person is argued in court. Both sides of the policy or case are presented so that citizens or jurors can make up their own minds.

A second beneficial aspect of Gorgias was his contribution to the psychology of rhetoric in his work called *The Defense of Helen*.[4] As the catalyst of the Trojan War, Helen of Sparta was the most notorious female figure of Greek mythology. Famed for her exceptional beauty, she evoked both admiration and loathing—especially loathing if one supposed that she had abandoned her Greek husband of her own free will, and plunged Greek communities into a devastating conflict. Gorgias composed his *Defense of Helen* to show that, whatever the circumstances of Helen's abandonment of Menelaus for the Trojan prince Paris, she should not be blamed because she was not a free agent. I need not summarize Gorgias's entire argument here. Its relevance to this chapter is twofold: his proof that Helen was innocent if she was persuaded by discourse *(logos)*, and the roles that body and soul play in his argument.

The Defense of Helen is the earliest surviving evidence for any Greek author's systematic use of a distinction between *soma* and *psyche*.[5] Gorgias's prose style is marked by antithesis and parallelism. These rhetorical devices are strongly at work in the way he uses the above terms. But more than rhetoric is involved. Gorgias incorporates a definite theory about the functions of body and soul. This theory is strikingly at odds with the subordination of body to soul recommended by Socrates, Plato, and Isocrates, who are all followed by the subsequent philosophical tradition. Sometimes Gorgias juxtaposes body and soul, and at other times he contrasts them. The overall effect is first, to emphasize the strength of the body and the power of beauty, and second, to represent the soul as impotent to resist both rhetorical persuasion and erotic attraction mediated by sight. Gorgias postulates a general principle, which Plato echoes in his dialogue with passionate opposition from Socrates. The principle is the unassailable supremacy of power:

> It is not in nature that the stronger be impeded by the weaker, but rather that the weaker be ruled and taken by the stronger, and that the stronger lead and the weaker follow."[6]

This principle is quite indifferent to all values except physical power.

The principle can be seen at work in the fact that Helen "by her single body united many men's bodies" inasmuch as they gathered together to compete for her favors. Bodies, as Gorgias says elsewhere, are three-dimensional solids and they occupy place.[7] Helen's body, conforming to this definition, was so beautiful that it had the power to cause many other bodies to move together in pursuit of her. But bodies, according to Gorgias, do not need to be visible like Helen in order to have significant effects. Discourse itself or *logos* (taken to be uttered sounds) is only a small and invisible body, but it can have great power over a soul. Persuasive discourse can produce joy, stop fear, remove pain, and enhance pity. Poetry especially, or rhythmical discourse, affects the soul when the soul hears about the success or failure of actions, and also when the soul hears about other people's actions and "bodies" *(somata),* meaning their lives or themselves.

Gorgias does not suggest that any soul has the power to resist persuasive discourse completely. On the contrary, he takes such discourse to be a kind of witchcraft that causes the soul to make mistakes and impairs its capacity for judgment *(doxa).*[8] Another model Gorgias uses to signify the power of rhetoric over the soul is the influence of drugs or medications. Such things have powerful effects on the body; similarly, discourse affects the soul's structure *(taxis).*

Gorgias does not confine his treatment of the soul's weakness to its liability to be persuaded by discourses.

GREEK MODELS OF MIND AND SELF

When Helen fell in love with Paris, she was presumably overwhelmed not only by what he said to her to persuade her to leave her Spartan home for Troy with him, but also by his beauty. Gorgias accordingly continues his defense of Helen by arguing that love inspired by the beloved's beauty has irresistible power over the soul. The soul is "molded" by what it sees. Some sights disturb the soul and cause people to panic, but artificial bodies like paintings or statues or ornaments generate pleasure; sexually attractive bodies transmit erotic passion to the soul. In such cases, Gorgias implies, external bodies can entrap souls so strongly that they become quite unable to resist. The power of persuasion, then, though strictly a function of rhetorically charged discourse, also extends to the general effect that beautiful bodies have on souls.

Gorgias begins his *Defense of Helen* by describing a soul's ornament as wisdom and that of discourse as truth, but his ensuing argument shows the irony of these accolades. Rather than truth, Gorgias takes persuasion and deception to be the salient features of discourse, with fallible opinion and manipulation as their characteristic effect on the soul. Just as the soul is the locus and target of persuasion, it is also the seat of pleasure and pain, or desire and fear. The soul makes judgments *(doxai)*, but these may as easily

BODIES, SOULS, AND PERSUASION

or more easily be false as true. Rather than being autonomous opinions, *doxai,* as interpreted by Gorgias, seem to be simply the outcome of whatever discourse the soul finds most persuasive.

If we compare this view of *psyche* with the Homeric material surveyed in Chapter 1, it seems to correspond to the uses of the term *thumos* rather than *phrenes* or *nous.* These latter words in Homer have stronger cognitive connotations. Far from elevating *psyche* to be a human being's natural or normative ruler, Gorgias treats it as a purely instrumental faculty, reactive to how the body is impacted from outside. In this conception the Gorgianic *psyche* is completely antithetical to the Socratic ideal as formulated by Plato. Far from being a capacity to initiate long-term goals, weigh up alternatives, and resist foolish impulses, it is always emotionally at risk, lacking in any secure reasoning and rationality.

Gorgias gave theoretical expression to what was certainly the zeitgeist as registered by Thucydides, the period's most hardheaded commentator. His *History of the Peloponnesian War* is packed with examples of the way powerful speeches can convince people to act against their best interests or throw conventional restraints aside. Gorgias's analysis of *psyche* in *Defense of Helen* also fits the way Herodotus, the

GREEK MODELS OF MIND AND SELF

epoch's other great historian, represents the mind-set of the Persian King Xerxes when this figure is trying to decide whether to invade Greece (*History* 7, 8-18). Xerxes asks two of his advisers for counsel. One of them urges him to undertake this war, while the other urges caution. Xerxes finds the cautious advice more persuasive. But when he goes to bed, he has a dream that urges him to invade Greece after all or suffer terrifying consequences. He tells this dream to his advisers. The cautious one recommends him to ignore the dream. In response, Xerxes tells him to put on the king's clothes, sleep in the king's bed, and see if he has the same imperious dream. After rationalistic objections to this outrageous command, the cautious adviser complies and is, of course, visited by the same dream. To which he responds by now admitting that his earlier warning was mistaken. Xerxes, then, proceeds disastrously with his invasion.

This story is almost certainly a fiction. But it suggests a similar view of the soul or mind to the one that Gorgias presents in his *Defense of Helen*. Xerxes does not think things out for himself. He asks others to do the thinking for him. He goes along with whatever course of action appears to him the more persuasive at the moment, whether it comes from his

BODIES, SOULS, AND PERSUASION

advisers or from dreams. His mind is the persuadable faculty that Gorgias calls *psyche*.

Gorgias does not say that human beings are composites of body and soul, but that is clearly what he implies. To that extent he agrees with Isocrates, but rather than give the soul authority over the body in his *Defense of Helen*, Gorgias reverses these assessments by giving the body authority over the soul. Plato's dialogue *Gorgias* is not simply an attack on Gorgias's claims for the value of rhetoric but an equally strong rejection of Gorgias's psychological assumptions in the *Helen*. To Gorgias's defense of Helen's innocence and impotence, Plato opposes the soul's potential autonomy and its priority over the body in a proper understanding of human nature.

As we now leave Gorgias for Plato, I should not let the impression stand that Gorgias himself defended Helen's psychological weakness as a universal human characteristic. At the end of the *Helen* he even calls the work a joke. Gorgias was the earliest Greek author on record to use master and slave as metaphors for self-control, as in the expression "mastery over pleasure" and "enslavement to pleasure." This metaphor, as I remarked before, was one of Plato's favorite devices for expressing the proper relation of soul to body, with the role of master assigned to the former and the role of slave to the latter. Gorgias drew on this metaphor to explain, in another of his speeches, that the Greek hero Palamedes could not have committed the crime he was accused of because he was *not* enslaved to pleasure.[9] We can see from Gorgias's surviving work that he liked to try out ideas, even contradictory ideas, without necessarily subscribing to them. In Plato's eyes, however, this characteristic will have intensified his view of Gorgias as a mere rhetorician, unwilling to take responsibility for the damaging effects his speeches may have on an impressionable audience.

Plato's subordination of the body to the soul, as we have seen from my quotation of Isocrates, was not a novel idea in its time. What was revolutionary about Plato's treatment of it is the way Plato drew on the body both as an analogy for the soul, as we have already seen, and as a contrast to it. Probably the earliest sign of Plato's thinking along these lines occurs at that point in the dialogue *Crito* (46d–48a) where Socrates seeks to prove that, in questions about how one should act, the only relevant criterion is justice, and not what popular opinion takes to be right or wrong. Here we have an implicit contrast between the value of truth and the value of mere opinion, true or false, which is the state of mind that rhetoric seeks to produce according to Gorgias's use of *doxa* in his *Defense of Helen*.

The foundation of Socrates's proof is the following argument. If you want to be in good bodily condition, you do not take just anyone's advice on diet or training but the advice of those who are experts. No one wants to live with a ruined body, and so people put themselves under the charge of doctors and gymnastic trainers. By analogy, if you want your moral self to be healthy, you should take the advice of someone who is genuinely knowledgeable about justice, and not follow the guidance of those who merely think that they know what is right. The phrase "your moral self" is not in the Greek text. I use it, in order to refer to what Socrates here calls "the thing that is harmed by injustice and helped by justice."

Why does Plato use this elaborate expression rather than call the "thing" *psyche* or soul? The circumlocution must be Plato's sign that at this early date in his literary career, Greek readers do not automatically associate the word *psyche* with health and morality, and are hardly familiar with the explicit analogy between bodily wellness and psychic flourishing. Even the historical Socrates may not have made the connection so exactly. On the evidence of Plato's *Apology*, in the passage quoted above, Socrates prioritized the soul's well-being above that of the body. That is clearly a step toward the health analogy, but it does not go all the way.

Gorgias had drawn connections between body and soul by comparing the effect of drugs on the body with the effect of persuasive speech on the soul. That is an arresting and insightful comparison, but it does not suggest a direct analogy between bodily health and a just soul. This Platonic analogy is a momentous idea as soon as we reflect on the traditional association of *psyche* with the principle of life. If your life is due to the way your *psyche* animates your body, and if your *psyche* can be in a truly good condition only if it is just, then you need to be just in order to have a truly good life. Much of Plato's writing is devoted to developing this argument. Before proceeding to details, I want to make some general points about the body/soul analogy and the analogy of physical health and moral health.

In reading Plato, we are constantly reminded of the importance of gymnastics in Greek culture. Plato's milieu was obsessed with physical prowess, as is evident from the prestige attached to victory in the annual Panhellenic games, artistic representations

BODIES, SOULS, AND PERSUASION

of athletes, and the linguistic expression *kalos kagathos,* conjoining "good" and "beautiful" in the designation of elite Athenian males. The culture was so far from being obsessed with the value of philosophy that in the *Gorgias,* Plato puts Socrates in the position of being mocked for his devotion to its pursuit.[10] Athletics and physical training provided Plato with the most obvious analogy he could find for elaborating his own ideal of a life devoted to training and perfecting the mind as distinct from the body. To some extent we have inherited Plato's categories of thought with our current interests in what we call mental health. Physicians and therapists trained in this field seek to have salutary effects on their patients' behavior. They hope to help their patients function well at home and in society, but modern practitioners hardly think of themselves as having the expertise to train people precisely in moral health. Plato sought to prove that there is such a thing as objective moral health, and that this is a necessary accompaniment of genuine mental health. The health of the soul, as understood by Plato, was both an intellectual achievement and a virtue of character. If you could truly understand the nature of justice, you would also understand that justice is as good and necessary for your wellness, under the aspect of your soul, as good food and exercise are necessary for the health of your body.

The body/soul analogy and contrast, once it was launched on its way, shaped Greek philosophy ever after. It is evident in the idea of a philosophical education as therapeutic, in the idea that faults of character are diseases of the soul, and in the idea that moral virtues are the manifestation of a soul that is stable, robust, and as glistening as the sheen on an athlete's well-toned body. The ideal of mental/moral health promoted the importance of systematic exercise *(askesis)*, meaning that living well requires constant practice, self-examination, and self-discipline. *Askesis* was an entirely different human ideal from the aristocratic, militaristic, and competitive values of Homer, where, as we saw in Chapter 1, sharp distinctions were not drawn between people's bodies and souls, or between their physical and mental attributes.

I have suggested that Plato's Socratic elevation of the soul over the body was decisively shaped by his wish to oppose the cultural and political influence of rhetoric and its threats, as he judged them, to autonomy and moral responsibility. Another way of stating the same point is to emphasize Plato's unremitting opposition to the educational program

BODIES, SOULS, AND PERSUASION

offered by the fifth-century BCE sophists, in addition to Gorgias, which focused on training in rhetoric. The most celebrated of the sophists was Protagoras. At the beginning of his dialogue named after this man, Plato has Socrates issue the following warning to a youth who is gung-ho to sit at Protagoras's feet:

> Are you aware of the kind of danger to which you are going to expose your soul ... There is much greater risk in purchasing lessons than in buying food stuffs. In that case or in buying things to drink you can carry them away from the store and the seller in containers. Before taking them into your body by eating and drinking, you can store them at home and deliberate, with the help of an expert, on what to eat and drink, how much and at what time. So the purchase is not very risky. But you cannot carry lessons away in a different container from yourself. Once you have paid for them you have to put them directly into your soul.

Socrates' warning is histrionically expressed for comic effect. But Plato's point hits home. Lectures and books, as he says elsewhere, cannot talk back, in the manner of Socratic question and answer. Advertising works, not because we are quite clear about what its products will do for us, but because of how they are packaged, or as Plato puts it, by how we take them into our souls.[11]

The discussion in the *Gorgias* has reached the point at which the defender of Gorgias named Callicles has argued that the best and happiest life is freedom to indulge one's appetites with no restraint. Socrates counters this position by proposing the exact opposite—that self-restraint is essential to a good life (491e). He then (493a) makes a pun on the Greek word for a jar *(pithos)* and the word for being persuadable *(pithanos)* and applies the pun to "the part of the soul where the appetites are." The jar, we are told, cannot be filled because it constantly leaks. By analogy, Socrates proposes that unrestrained people are like a leaky jar because their appetites are never satisfied: they are constantly in the position of being persuaded by their desires.

This passage is clearly meant to recall Socrates's description of rhetoric as a type of persuasive discourse that is aimed at merely "flattering" or pandering to the souls of an audience. The rhetorician is not equipped with the skill that could genuinely benefit those who hear him by improving their souls and their characters. Rather, he has a technique that is aimed at merely giving them momentary pleasure (that is, satisfying their desires) without concern for what is best. In this same context, just before mentioning the soul's appetites, Socrates alludes to a saying, probably originating with Heraclitus, that goes: "Who knows whether living is really being dead, and being dead is living?" Socrates then mentions a further saying, perhaps voiced by Pythagoras or Empedocles, that our body is our tomb (which is a pun on the words *soma* and *sema*).

The body/tomb equation, and the inversion of the conventional contrast of life and death, anticipates Socrates's startling proposition in Plato's dialogue called *Phaedo*, that philosophy, because it requires the philosopher to detach his soul from his body, is training for dying and being dead, even when one is still physically alive (64a). As we shall see at the end of this chapter, the Socratic thesis comparing philosophy to a death-like condition assigns appetitive desires and failures of knowledge to the body as distinct from the soul. Here in the *Gorgias*, probably an earlier composition, Plato does not treat the body so negatively. He draws on bodily conditions, as in the dialogue called the *Crito,* to exploit their value for explaining the health of the soul. So, Socrates says (*Gorgias* 505a):

> Doctors generally allow healthy persons to satisfy their appetites for food and drink, as much as they like, but virtually never permit that in the case of the sick.... Is it not the same with the soul? As long as the soul is in a poor condition, because it is foolish and lacks control, and is unjust and unholy, it needs to have its desires checked and not be allowed to have anything except things that will improve it.

The parallel between bodily and psychic health had already been prepared for by recourse to the concepts of order, structure, and harmony (503e). A true rhetorician, meaning a statesman who was genuinely concerned about the moral health of citizens, would seek to address their souls with discourses aimed at their acquiring justice and moderation, and removing the corresponding faults. Socrates then infers that the equivalent of health for the soul, the condition that the soul requires in order to possess order, harmony, and structure, is a combination of justice and moderation.[12]

BODIES, SOULS, AND PERSUASION

A soul with these qualities must be in the opposite state from one that lacks self-restraint and seeks to satisfy all appetitive desires. Rather than identify power with such a life, as Callicles had advocated, Socrates proposes that order, structure, and harmony constitute power in the universe at large (the macrocosm) and generate a truly good and happy life for human individuals (the microcosm).

Gorgias had argued in *The Defense of Helen* that souls are as powerless to resist persuasive speeches as bodies are powerless to resist the drugs they may be given. This is a bleakly deterministic view of human nature. Plato's rejoinder in the dialogue named after Gorgias invites us to consider that souls are not simply appetitive and liable to be persuaded by the mere encounter with rhetorical skill. That position fails to take account of the fact that souls, and therefore human lives, willfully go astray by failing to acknowledge that wrongdoing is supremely harmful to the wrongdoer. To underline this principle, Socrates at the end of the dialogue represents the unjust and unrestrained soul, even when stripped of its flesh and bones, as if it were a horribly scarred and wounded body, twisted out of all healthy alignment.

GREEK MODELS OF MIND AND SELF

In the *Gorgias,* Plato does not explain the exact nature of the body or the soul. He uses these terms to distinguish between two generic categories—a good and well-trained human condition (ensuing from gymnastics and philosophy, as it were) and a condition that is deviant and poorly trained (the outcome of poor diet, mere cosmetics, and a superficial rhetorical education). A well-trained and healthy body has, as its mental and moral correlate, a well-disciplined and well-ordered soul, with corresponding deficiencies for the ill-trained body and the ill-trained soul.

What is it that enables souls, according to Plato, to resist beguiling rhetoric and achieve the autonomy that Gorgias had seemed to withhold from them? How should readers of the *Gorgias,* sympathetic to Socrates, negotiate their human condition as embodied souls? Plato does not fully answer that question in this dialogue. To end the present chapter, I turn to the responses that Plato ascribes to Socrates in the dialogue *Phaedo,* named after one of Socrates's main associates.

The *Phaedo* exhibits Socrates in prison, conversing with his friends on the day that will end with his execution. We can infer that Plato had already written

BODIES, SOULS, AND PERSUASION

the *Gorgias* because the *Phaedo* starts at the point where the *Gorgias* ends—the separation of body and soul at death. In the *Gorgias* Socrates opines that each of these separated things will retain its former qualities for a time at least, but he does not explicitly ascribe immortality to the soul. In the *Phaedo* Socrates undertakes to show why philosophers are not afraid of death. He repeats the statement that death is the separation of body and soul. In what follows he produces a series of complex arguments to prove that the soul is literally immortal and imperishable. During this lengthy argumentation Socrates treats body and soul quite differently from his procedure in the *Gorgias*. There, without setting one above the other, he presented body and soul in parallel, making neither of them good or bad in itself. Now, in the *Phaedo,* Socrates contrasts body and soul in the most extreme terms: bodies are visible, changeable, impure, and perishable; souls are invisible, incorporeal, immortal, and potentially perfectible and divine.

This is not the place to investigate the dialogue's many arguments for the soul's immortality. Plato may not have regarded any of them as fully cogent. I am not even sure that he was fully committed to a belief in the soul's literal immortality. Whenever he describes the soul's afterlife he uses myth and allegory. In more theoretical contexts he sometimes qualifies immortality with the phrase "as far as possible." What I am sure about is Plato's total commitment to the metaphysical and evaluative contrasts he draws between body and soul.

The premise of his argument is quite simply that the body *as such* has negative value and that the soul *as such* has positive value. What I mean by adding "as such" is that these contrasting values are inherent in the entities themselves, irrespective of whose body and soul is in question. Plato disparages the body for many reasons, including its instability, its neediness, and its "desires, which are the source of war and faction and fighting" (66c). The principal outcome is enhancement of the status of the soul, or what he takes to be the essentially mental and moral identity of the self or person. In the course of establishing this position, Plato sets up extreme antitheses between the physical and sensual side of human nature and the intellectual and spiritual side. No one, to the best of our knowledge, had done that before, or at least had not done it with Plato's precision and virtuosity. This antithesis, for better or worse, is the strongest mark of Plato's influence on Western culture.

The main contrast is worked out by a whole series of oppositions between the desires of a philosopher on the one hand and the desires of ordinary people on the other hand. Ordinary people are presumed to be out-and-out hedonists, devoted to the pleasures of eating, drinking, and sex, and to wanting external things for their bodies like fine clothes and ornaments. The philosopher, on the other hand, tries to detach himself from the body in order to focus attention as far as possible only on his soul. Why does he do that? Plato's answer to this question takes us into the heart of his outlook on reality and the resources he attributes to human beings for understanding reality. The philosopher tries to marginalize his body because he finds it an impediment to his quest for truth. The bodily senses of sight, hearing, and so forth are taken to be too inaccurate and unreliable to yield any purchase on truth, while the desires that the body generates are a further distraction from thought. The philosopher's task is to focus on reasoning as distinct from perceiving. Socrates expresses this extreme intellectualist position as follows:

> The clearest knowledge will surely be attained by one who approaches the true realities as far as possible by thought, and thought alone, not permitting sight or any other sense to intrude

> upon his thinking... one who gets rid, as
> much as possible, of eyes and ears and, broadly
> speaking, of the body altogether, knowing that
> when the body is the soul's partner it confuses
> the soul and prevents it from coming to possess
> truth and intelligence. (*Phaedo* 65e)

This is an extraordinary recommendation. Elsewhere, even in this dialogue itself, Plato acknowledges that our bodily senses are indispensable for equipping our minds with information as we try to arrive at the nonempirical understanding of ultimate truths. Here Socrates seems to say that we would be better off, even as embodied beings, without sense organs. This of course is hyperbole, a dramatically exaggerated way of highlighting the faculty and value of abstract thought.

In the *Gorgias* the perils of persuasion were rhetoric's potentiality to corrupt souls with the idea that the best course in life is to fulfill one's desires without paying heed to justice or order in the soul. In the *Phaedo* Plato transfers the perils of persuasion to the body and the body's demands to have its hedonistic desires satisfied. The body's desires, according to this view, are also the reason for social disorder and war, in the quest for wealth as the means to satisfy them. The negative influence of the body provides Plato with an answer to the question of why human beings may be attracted to injustice, the great theme of the *Gorgias* to which that dialogue provided no explicit answer. However, as Plotinus recognized, Plato's main focus in the *Phaedo* is intellectual rather than ethical.[13] The philosopher tries to live simply in his soul or mind in order to maximize his resources for understanding the unchanging nature of ultimate reality. Plato does not fully explain why the philosopher has this motivation. It does not fit his characterization of Socrates's missionary zeal to reform the values of the Athenian populace. On the evidence of the *Phaedo,* the theoretical life of the mind was Plato's ultimate focus.[14]

The extreme dualism of Plato's *Phaedo* raises many questions. As early as Homer, Greek authors had recognized that human beings consist of such parts as flesh, blood, bones and limbs, and other kinds of parts that are the source and location of thoughts, feelings, and desires. They recognized, implicitly, that the body necessarily influences the mind, and the mind the body. If that were not so, how could our thoughts and feelings generate our actions? This view of human nature was not dualistic but psychosomatic. Plato, in the work I have just been considering, acknowledges that the body affects the soul, but rather than explaining how this happens he prefers to view body and soul as unhappily conjoined during life, treating the soul at its best as a purely intellectual capacity in detachment as far as possible from its bodily accompaniment.

In Chapter 4 we will see how Plato modified this model by proposing that the philosopher's project is not so much to achieve mastery over the body but rather to establish the rule of reason within the soul, which he now credits with distinct capacities of intellect, spirit, and appetite. According to this more complex model (which I touched on at the end of Chapter 1), the desires and distractions Plato attributed to the body in the *Phaedo* are now to be viewed as features of the soul itself. In place of body/soul dualism what will chiefly interest Plato in this further stage of his thinking is a distinction between rational and nonrational desires.

Outside Platonism, the philosophers who came after Plato were not disposed to think of body and soul as two distinct things in the manner of the *Phaedo*. For Aristotle body and soul are two aspects of one thing, corresponding to matter on the one hand and form on the other hand. In Aristotle's view, the

BODIES, SOULS, AND PERSUASION

human body (or, rather, any living thing's body), is not intelligible as the complex structure that it is without the soul as its activating principle, nor is the soul intelligible as something that could exist apart from the body because the soul is precisely the essence of an organic body.[15] In Epicureanism and Stoicism, the soul is a particular type of physical structure within the flesh-and-blood body. Because the soul itself, according to these philosophers, is physical, it can animate the body by the physical properties of motion and contact.[16]

These later philosophers were not tempted by Plato's metaphysical dualism, but in their theories of value they strongly reveal his influence. All of them agreed that human nature should be analyzed in terms of a distinction between body and soul. They also agreed that the soul is essentially the most important and the most valuable aspect of human nature. For Aristotle the best human life is characterized by virtuous activity of soul. For Epicurus the pleasures of the soul are preferable to the pleasures of the body. In Stoicism, happiness is excellence of soul. One could write the history of Greek philosophy in terms of the superiority of soul to body. That is Plato's legacy.

Further Reading

Dodds, E. R. (1959), ed., *Plato, Gorgias* (Oxford).

Gagarin, M., and Woodruff, P. (1995), eds., *Early Greek Political Thought from Homer to the Sophists* (Cambridge, UK).

Gallop, D. (1975), *Plato: Phaedo* (Oxford).

Holmes, B. (2010), *The Symptom and the Subject: The Emergence of the Physical Body in Ancient Greece* (Princeton).

Irwin, T. (1979), *Plato: Gorgias* (Oxford).

North, H. (1966), *Sophrosyne: Self-Knowledge and Self-Restraint in Greek Literature* (Ithaca).

Robinson, T. (1995), *Plato's Psychology* (Toronto).

Wagner, E. (2001), ed., *Essays on Plato's Psychology* (Lanham, MD).

4

THE POLITICIZED SOUL
AND THE RULE OF REASON

IN CHAPTER 3 we saw how Plato uses the distinction between body and soul to develop such antitheses as mortal/ immortal, physical health/moral health, opinion/knowledge, appearance/reality, disorder/harmony, change/stability. Such dualism is evident throughout his philosophy, but we should not conclude from this fact that Plato was committed to a single model of the mind/body relation and the structure of human identity. While his thinking about these things regularly draws on these antitheses, the details of his psychology and physiology are always shaped by the dialogical context. In the case of the *Gorgias,* that context is rhetoric, while in the *Phaedo* it is Socrates's approaching death and expectation of a superior life for his disembodied soul. In the dialogue to which I come now the context is the politics and authority that best suit human society.

The work that will chiefly concern us here is the *Republic,* which is regularly acknowledged to be Plato's philosophical and literary masterpiece. Like the *Gorgias* and the *Phaedo,* the *Republic* concludes with a myth of the soul's postmortem destiny, but this dialogue is on a much larger scale both in sheer size and in conceptual range than either of these works. Besides politics and ethics, the *Republic* includes remarkable discussions of education, literature, aesthetics, theology, metaphysics, and epistemology. This range of topics, vast though it is, does not prevent the work from having a unitary theme, whether we give it its standard title or the title *On Justice,* by which it was also known in antiquity. Republic—*politeia* in Greek—is the Latinized term for what we today call society or the state. At one level Plato's project is to examine the conditions under which a political community could be organized, from the outside as it were, so as best to provide for the well-being of all its members. Under this description the *Republic* treats the optimal conditions for government, economic success, and security.

Citizens, however, are individual human beings. As such, according to Plato's standard way of analyzing

POLITICIZED SOUL AND REASON

human nature, they each consist of a body and a soul, with the soul presumed to be the thing within us that organizes and has charge of the body. Plato, accordingly, does not pursue his project in the *Republic* simply in terms of identifying the best constitution or form of government, with that taken to be something external to the lives and consciousness of the citizens. On the contrary, he develops the main argument of the dialogue in ways that treat politics and psychology as two aspects of a single investigation, and he does so for the following reason. An ideal society must have the best possible system of government, education, and social practices. In order for that to work as a system that is both effective and fair, it needs to be compatible with the interests, consent, and aptitudes of the persons, who make up the state as its diverse living parts. External political order is to be mirrored by internal psychological order. Hence the virtues of the state as a whole are to have their counterpart in the virtues of the individual citizens.

Scholars often ask which topic is primary for Plato. Is it politics or is it psychology? Does he model his utopian state on a theory about the structure of the soul, or is the theory concerning the soul's structure and good organization founded upon the organization of the ideal state? In the sequence of topics, the discussion of the state comes first, and ostensibly prepares the ground for the treatment of the soul. Having been introduced to three distinct citizen classes for the state, we are invited to see whether an analogous division pertains to the souls of individual persons. This is found to be true. State and soul are structurally alike inasmuch as each of them has three distinct parts that, for the good of the whole (whether the state or the soul), must be organized so that the part best qualified to rule is in charge, and the parts best qualified to be secondary are assigned their subordinate functions.[1]

To pursue the question of priority further, let us next review the respective parts of the state and the soul. In the case of the state, the three parts are the governing guardians, their assistant military auxiliaries, and the workers who supply food and other practical services. Applying this system to the soul, we are offered, as analogous parts, the calculative or rational part *(logistikon),* the spirited or energizing part *(thumoeides),* and the appetitive part *(epithumetikon).* This latter part, we should notice, is not taken to be responsible for all the soul's desires, but only for its basic appetites for food, drink, and so forth. As such, this part of the soul corresponds to the appetitive role Plato assigns to the body in the *Phaedo*.

POLITICIZED SOUL AND REASON

Plato's division of the soul into three parts is based not only on the project of achieving parallelism to the tripartite structure of the state but also on independent reasons concerning human motivations. We will study those reasons in due course. My immediate concern, however, is to draw attention to something more basic to the psychological theory, something so obvious that it is often passed over without comment—namely, the most important shared feature of the soul/state analogy beyond the common property of tripartite and functional division. I refer to the distinction between a rightfully *ruling* part and rightfully *subordinate* parts. Plato's *Republic* as a whole is premised on the principle that in the universe, in politics, and in the soul, one thing, and one thing alone, is properly qualified to control and to exercise authority over everything else. That one thing is reason or reasoning, expressed in Greek by means of the noun *logismos,* the adjective *logistikos,* and the verb *logizesthai.*

Let us now focus upon these two notions, proper authority and reason. The notion of proper authority is plainly derived from the political sphere. In proposing that souls need internal governance in order to function well, Plato is applying politics to the soul. The notion of authority or rule *(arche)* presupposes the ideas of superiority and subordination, as of a governing body to that which is governed, or of a master to a slave. Plato, we can be sure, drew heavily upon his own political experience in explaining the conditions of souls at their best and at their worst, including strong antipathy to Athenian democracy and still greater antipathy to tyranny.[2] What Plato's political experience did not provide him with is the notion of reason and reasoning, as expressed in the words *logismos* and so forth. In fact the most striking single feature of Plato's political theory is his proposal that states can function well only if they are *rationally* governed or, as he says in the *Republic,* if they are ruled by *philosophers*—that is to say, lovers of wisdom, understanding, and exact knowledge. He had found that situation lamentably lacking in Athenian politics as it was actually practiced, with the trial and execution of Socrates, as an enemy of the state, its most flagrant error.

Before asking what precisely Plato means by reason and reasoning, let us return to the now familiar idea that people's souls and bodies have, or should have, a relationship to one another of ruler and subject. Plato was hardly the first or the only contemporary Greek thinker to apply a political model to the normative structure of human beings. As we saw in Chapter 3, Isocrates (probably at more or less this time) had said that it is the function of the soul to deliberate about public and personal matters, and the function of the body to serve the soul's decisions (*Antidosis* 180). Quite similarly, before Plato begins to develop the state/soul analogy in the *Republic,* he gives Socrates a brief argument, to the effect that the function of souls is twofold: first, to rule and deliberate, and second, to live.[3] To rule and deliberate well, a soul needs justice, and likewise, Socrates infers, it needs justice to live well. This argument, very short though it is, has a programmatic function in the dialogue because it connects good rule, justice, a good life, and a good soul. However, Socrates in this short argument does not explicitly connect good rule with reason and reasoning, nor had Isocrates explicitly made that connection when he asserted that it is the soul's job to control the body by means of deliberation. One can deliberate, meaning investigate what it is best to do, without necessarily arriving at decisions that satisfy norms of reasoning, consistency, or precise calculation. In modern deliberative bodies, ideology and emotion typically trump criteria grounded on evidence and the greatest happiness of the greatest number.

I want to emphasize the significant novelty of Plato's associating good rule with reason or reasoning, in Greek *logismos* and *logizesthai*. How we are to understand reason in the *Republic* will be fully explained only when we read the central books, which seem to take us far away from politics and psychology. There Plato delves into metaphysics and epistemology, prefacing that discussion with the proposition that ideal and abstract goodness is the world's first principle.[4] Understanding that principle, he argues, is indispensable if a community is to have its own share of goodness. Hence the absolute good becomes the ultimate subject of study by philosopher rulers, who are to govern the state by the rule of reason. As preparation for such study, these persons are required to become expert mathematicians. I can pass over the details here in order to make my main point: reason for Plato is not restricted to mathematics, but mathematics gives us the best guide for elucidating what he means by reason. For Plato good rule is the application of reason, where reason involves making correct calculations concerning what is best for all concerned, whether the scope of that is the individual soul or the state at large. Plato's understanding of reason in general is mathematical in the sense that reason's goal is unequivocal truth and exactitude. The soul's rule of reason, as Plato understands it, is neither probabilistic nor is it an instrumental means-ends calculus. It is the application to politics of an exact faculty of measurement or, better, an exact faculty of establishing harmonious proportions.

The genealogy of Plato's politicized concept of rationality, surprisingly enough, has not been exhaustively researched. Suffice it to say here that its earliest antecedents include Heraclitus's interests in measure (*logos* and *metron*) as philosophical inquiry's explanatory tool, and the mathematical harmonics and numerical ratios attributed to Pythagoras and his followers. By the time Plato wrote the *Republic*, according to the standard chronology of his works, he had already elucidated knowledge and craftsmanship *(techne)* in terms of the guidance these faculties confer on their possessors' ability to lead and to rule.[5] Very likely, this notion was one of Socrates's principal legacies. It is improbable, however, that Socrates had the kind of mathematical interests that were conducive to Plato's specifically mathematical notion of reason's rule in virtue of the capacity to *calculate* or *measure* what is best for states and souls.

GREEK MODELS OF MIND AND SELF

Whether politics should be the art of the possible or the craft of what is best, and how reason should pertain to government—these are questions I leave aside. My purpose here is purely historical, to lay out, as clearly as I can, the creativity, novelty, and imagination at work in Plato's politicization of the soul. The *rule* of reason is a phrase we ourselves can hardly experience with the power and freshness that it must have had when Plato enunciated it. For us it is not a particularly striking expression, perhaps no more than a dead metaphor, like enslavement to desire. In order to grasp its significance in Plato's political model of the soul, we need to spend a few moments of reflection on the Greek politics of his time.

By politics I mean forms of social organization set out in constitutions codified by laws, with documented procedures for the distribution of offices, control of power, and administration of justice. In Plato's own day two such systems predominated, democracy and oligarchy, but the Greeks were also familiar with one-man rule, either by hereditary succession (monarchy) or by seizure of power (tyranny). Because Greek city-states numbered their citizens in the thousands rather than the millions, their inhabitants were much more closely involved

POLITICIZED SOUL AND REASON

in political life than is the case in most modern communities. Another feature of Greek society was the relative frequency of civic discord *(stasis)*, which could culminate in revolution and a sudden change of constitution, from democracy to oligarchy, or vice versa, or the imposition of a tyranny.[6]

Plato draws on these different political systems when he explains how the ideal state would decline from its utopian best to its despotic worst.[7] He argues that this political decline would be accompanied by, or rather would be the outward sign of, a progressive psychological decline in the structure of the citizens' souls. Rather than being ruled by reason, souls would progressively degenerate to the point where their worst faculty—nonrational, purely appetitive desire—becomes completely dominant. In order to come to terms with Plato's politicization of the soul, we need to recognize that he was not making use of a familiar metaphor, when recommending *the rule of reason*. He was almost certainly drawing very directly and originally on his own political experience.

One way to see that is to notice the absence of any such political model for mental states in Homer. As I remarked in Chapter 1, Homer set the scene for much of Plato's thinking about the soul and mental capacities. In the very context where Plato starts to politicize the soul (*Republic* 4.441b), he quotes the line (*Odyssey* 20.17) that reads: "Odysseus struck his chest, and rebuked his heart." Homer has been describing the hero's strong impulse to punish the girlfriends of the men who have courted Penelope in his absence, and how, with a great struggle, he resists that impulse. We can share Plato's view that Homer is here representing conflicting desires—the instant impulse to exact punishment versus the prudent desire to wait for the right moment—but Homer does not actually describe Odysseus's mental state as a conflict between reason and anger, much less as a struggle between different parts of the soul. Nor is it the case that Homer models mental states on the political notions of ruling and being ruled. For that to be possible, an author would need to be familiar with politics in a way that Homer, or at least Homeric epic, was not. There are kings and princes in the *Iliad* and *Odyssey,* but constitutional government and different forms of political organization were still in the future.[8]

Because Plato is such a powerful writer, it is easy to overlook his metaphors, and to take his models of the soul to be a natural and timelessly appropriate way to write about mental experience. In fact the *rule* of reason, like *enslavement* to passion, is an expression that directly reflects social realities of specific times and places, as is always occurring in metaphorical language. New expressions for the mind are a constant phenomenon, reflecting changes in human experience and everyday life. Today we frequently resort to technology for our mind metaphors, as when we describe someone as screwed up, wired, spaced out, dynamic, overcharged, pressured, or running on all cylinders. Earlier cultures have proposed religious or cosmological metaphors such as devilish, saintly, lunatic (meaning moonstruck), and so forth. If there is an interesting difference between Plato's political models and such later metaphors as these, it lies in Plato's consistently normative outlook. What I mean is Plato's conviction that there is only one objectively excellent way of life, consisting in reason's rule, but many deviant ways.

I now turn to the question of how Plato establishes the soul's possession of reason as both a distinct part and as the part that is naturally best and most authoritative. To gauge the importance of this question, we need only remind ourselves that human rationality, at least as the essential cause of goodness, has been hugely under challenge in modern times.

Whether we think back to the Scots philosopher David Hume, with his view that reason is and should be only the slave of the passions, or to the struggle that people and states continue to have to achieve peace and happiness, Plato's confidence in the benevolence of reason is something we need to interrogate very strongly if we think that his philosophy of mind and his understanding of human nature are real possibilities for us. Was he taking much too much for granted? In order to respond to this challenge, we should look very closely at the way he arrives at the proposal that the soul has three parts, analogous to the guardians, auxiliaries, and workers of the ideal state.

His argument starts by establishing that the soul has at least two parts.[9] The proof draws on the common experience of conflicting desires. At one and the same time and in the same respect, we are told, a person may both want and not want the same thing. Plato uses the example of someone who desires to drink but simultaneously tells himself not to drink. The subject of both desires is a single soul (or, as we could say, a single person), but how can a single soul have exactly opposite wants at the same time? The proposed answer, to account for the conflict, is that the single soul itself must contain or consist of distinct parts, each of which may want the opposite of what the other wants. According to this model we are divided or bifurcated selves.

We may doubt whether Plato's argument is fully cogent. It assumes too readily that conflicting desires are experienced simultaneously, rather than being experienced successively, so that the person oscillates rapidly between them without loss of unity. The Stoic philosophers proposed this oscillating model, and concluded that Plato was wrong to divide the soul into parts in order to account for conflicting desires.[10] For the Stoics, such conflicting desires indicate a weak character, which is imperfectly rational and unable to secure the stable rule of sound judgment. However, my interest here is not in the cogency of Plato's argument but in the way that he characterizes the supposedly distinct parts. He proposes that the desire for drink, in this conflicting case, must be an irrational or nonrational drive or craving, generated through "feelings and disorders," and that what resists this drive is the soul's rational or calculative faculty *(logistikon)*.

What is it about this faculty, according to Plato, that equips it to counteract a basic appetite, such as the desire to drink? He clearly assumes, for the context of his illustration, that resisting this desire is better than indulging it, so we can credit reason with a capacity to figure out what is *good* for the soul or the whole person in this case. Merely calculating that, though, would not be sufficient, we may suppose, to check a strong appetite, nor does Plato intend us to think so. Rather than construe reason as simply the capacity to calculate or to calculate what is best, Plato supposes that there are actual desires of reason.[11] What enables a soul to resist the thirsty appetite is the fact that, while desiring to drink, the soul also sees and desires something better, and motivates itself accordingly. In so acting, the soul's desire of reason is at work.

What is better, the argument leads us to think, is the long-term good of the soul, as a whole. The appetitive desire for drink does not involve any calculation or thought about good or bad. It is simply a craving. In the *Phaedo* Plato had attributed such cravings to the body. Now, with his political model of the soul, he situates the basic appetites within the soul itself. Instead of proposing that the best life is one in which persons ignore their bodies as much as possible, we are given the model of a self-governing soul, which governs the body by governing its own desires for bodily pleasures. Self-government, as Plato construes it on the political model, involves a ruling element

POLITICIZED SOUL AND REASON

and a ruled element. This Platonic self or soul is not a single entity, but a complex structure consisting of distinct motivating faculties or potentially opposing desires, desires of reason on the one hand and, on the other hand, nonrational desires such as our appetites for food, drink, and sex.

As envisioned by Plato here, the proper function of the soul's rational faculty is not only a capacity to moderate nonrational desires and resist harmful appetites, it is also the desire to rule the entire soul. Actual rulers or political officeholders are required to deliberate when they make public policy. As the soul's rightful ruler, reason deliberates by calculating what is best for the soul, thanks to its knowledge of the good. Plato, of course, was well aware of the fact that people often use reason for wrongful purposes. What I have just described is his account of a soul that makes reason sovereign as distinct from a soul that misuses reason to serve its appetites.

There is more to say about how reason is supposed to perform its ruling capacity. In preparation for that treatment, we need to analyze the third part of the soul in Plato's politicized model. I referred to this part before as the spirited or energizing part *(thumoeides),* noting that it is analogous in the soul to the military assistants of the guardians of the ideal state.

Plato tries to prove the existence of this soul part by arguing that our conscious experience involves not only reasoning and desiring—two mental processes that often conflict by simultaneously wanting completely opposite things—but also involves feelings as typified by anger. Because feelings are neither basic appetites (like the desires for food and drink) nor calculations, Plato infers that souls contain a part that is specifically responsible for this affective or emotional feature of our mental life.

In naming this part of the soul *thumoeides*, Plato chose a term that was unusual in this linguistic form, but very familiar in its first syllables. *Thumos*, as I explained in Chapter 1, is Homer's favorite word to identify the part of a person that is the agent or the location of thoughts, wishes, decisions, and feelings. Rather than draw distinctions between these mental occurrences, Homer very often attributes them all to a person's *thumos*. As I said when explaining all this before, *thumos* is as close as Homer comes to the notion of the mind that later Greeks generally refer to with the word *psyche*. To remind us, here are some Homeric instances: someone is said to have a harsh *thumos*, or to consider something in his *thumos*, or to have a *thumos* that is urging her on. By Plato's time

POLITICIZED SOUL AND REASON

this generic use of *thumos* was no longer current. The word was generally applied more restrictively to strong feeling, especially anger. That is how Plato introduces it in his division of the soul into three parts, where he imagines a person who gets angry and ashamed with himself for indulging a craving.[12]

At the same time Plato must have intended his readers to recall Homer's use of the term for the mind or soul of Homeric heroes. We can be certain of that for the following reason. In the *Republic* the decline of the ideal state starts when sons of the perfectly rational guardians succeed their fathers. The souls of these sons are not ruled by reason. In their case, the ruling element is the *thumos* part, whose dominance makes such people competitive honor-lovers.[13]

That expression is an unmistakable allusion to Homer's warrior culture. Glaucus, a character in the *Iliad* (6.208), describes the hero's motivation as "always to be best and to be superior to others." Honor, as manifested in competitive achievement, is the primary motivation of Homeric warriors. Fighting over honor sets the *Iliad* in motion, with the great quarrel over status between Agamemnon and Achilles. When such disputes occur in Homer, the voice of reason is scarcely heard. Honor and competition continued, of course, to be powerful aspects of Greek culture at the time of Plato himself. I am not suggesting that his treatment of the soul's *thumos* part was anachronistic. My point is that once we recognize the Homeric resonance of this element of the tripartite soul, we get a much clearer idea of what Plato was after in advocating the very different rule of reason. Competitive honor-lovers are not team players; they are out for themselves.

There is another clear sign that Plato's mind was on Homer when he identified the soul's competitive, honor-loving part with *thumos*. In his most striking image of how the three soul parts are combined in a single *psyche*, Plato invites us to imagine a sculptor making a model of the soul by representing it as a hybrid creature, consisting of a man, a lion, and "a many-headed beast," and inserting it into a body with the outward appearance of a man.[14] The man corresponds to the soul's rational part, and the many-headed beast is an image for the appetitive part with its multiple appetites for bodily pleasures. The lion is Plato's image for the *thumos* part. Not only does this recall Homeric heroes because of this soul part's competitive love of honor, it also recalls them because they are frequently likened in Homer to lions. Here, for instance, is how Homer describes the

Trojan prince Sarpedon, as he advances to attack the Greek army:

> He went like a mountain lion, starved for meat too long and his proud *thumos* urges him to make a raid on some sheep.... Just so, Sarpedon's *thumos* impelled him to assault the wall and break it down. (*Iliad* 12.299-308)

There are some thirty lion similes for warriors in the *Iliad*. Many of them, as in the one I have quoted, actually explain the lion/warrior's actions by mentioning his *thumos*.

Plato's recourse to Homer, for representing the emotional aspect of the soul, throws further light on the *Republic*'s emphasis on the rule of reason. As is well known, the citizens of Plato's utopia are not allowed to study Homer. This censorship of Greece's greatest literature, which was also the foundation of the culture's primary education, has always troubled and puzzled Plato's readers. Plato has two explicit reasons for banning the epic poet. One of these is Homer's quarrelsome and often immoral deities; the other reason is the emotional vulnerability of heroes, as when Achilles weeps over the death of Patroclus. The weeping Achilles is taken to be a bad role model for the utopia's citizens. What Plato does not say, but we can clearly supply as a third mark against Homer, is the fact that Homeric characters are driven by *thumos* rather than guided by reason.

Plato's "rule of reason" includes another non-Homeric notion, that of harmony. Once again we have a powerful metaphor applied to the elucidation of the mind, this time a metaphor derived from music. The Greek term *harmonia* means literally "fitting together." In the musical context of the time, this process involved tuning the strings of a lyre to yield the appropriate mode or melodic line. Plato draws upon this practice in order to explain the idea, to which he has now arrived with his politicized soul model, that the virtue of justice involves a structure of the soul whereby each part performs its proper function and does not interfere with the other parts. I translate *Republic* 4.442d:

> The just person ... being his own ruler, mentor, and friend, tunes the three elements just like three fixed points in a musical scale—top, bottom, and intermediate. And if there turn out to be any intervening elements, he must combine them all, and emerge as a perfect unity of diverse elements, self-disciplined and in harmony with himself.

POLITICIZED SOUL AND REASON

In the *Gorgias* (see Chapter 3) Plato had already contrasted the self-disciplined soul with a soul that allows free rein to all its appetites, but it is the politicized model from the *Republic* that explains the contrast most fully. As with politics, and as with reason construed as a faculty of exact calculation, so the notion of musical harmony gave Plato conceptual resources for modeling the mind that were hardly available to Homer.

Harmony, moreover, is basic to Plato's mental ideal throughout the *Republic*. Harmonics is one of the special fields of study that apprentice guardians must undertake as they are trained to become philosopher rulers. Numerous passages underline the connection between harmony and rationality. "Simple and moderate pleasures and desires" involve the guidance of *logismos* (431b). Here we have the quasi-mathematical idea of a soul that achieves balance in its feelings by subjecting them to appropriate calculation or proportion. Truth, we are asked to agree, is akin to proportion. In light of such passages, the rule of reason may be likened to a measuring device or standard. Not that we are to think of reason as simply an instrument or tool. Parts of the soul, as Plato construes them, are faculties and states of consciousness, which look beyond themselves to their desired objects, whether these are sensual pleasures, honor and victory, or truth and goodness. The rule of reason puts the lower two parts of the soul in their proper place, making them subordinate to the virtuous life of the entire soul, but it does not repress them. Rather, reason allows them the pleasures and satisfactions appropriate to their respective functions, provided that it takes charge of the entire complex and so enables it to live a fully harmonious life.[15]

Plato's politicized model of the soul reaches a rhetorical climax in the parallelism he draws between the ultimate decline of the state into tyranny and the analogous degeneration of the individual souls corresponding to each regime. After reason's rule has been supplanted by the rule of honor-loving *thumos* to create the political system of timocracy, the appetitive part of the soul dethrones *thumos,* in its turn; it replaces love of honor with appetite's rule manifested in desires for wealth, with the rational and *thumos* parts made subservient to these motivations. At the final stage of tyranny, the despot has thrown off all restraint. There is no order in his soul but only total anarchy.

This application of politics to the soul is a development from, and a philosophical improvement on, the body/soul dualism of Plato's earlier dialogues. That

POLITICIZED SOUL AND REASON

dualism facilitated a distinction between a properly ruling element (the soul) and a properly ruled element (the body). This model was also adaptable to an inversion of the proper hierarchy, as in the idea of the body enslaving the soul with its desires. However, the dualistic model does not clearly explain how two metaphysically different entities, a body and an incorporeal soul, can causally interact, and it is much too simple to convey the complexity of lived experience. With his politicized model of the soul, Plato attributes all experience to a single entity that we can call the mind or the person, and he achieves subtle explanations of the varieties of consciousness and temperament. We can debate the effectiveness of treating souls as analogous to political states and constitutions. But the notion that our minds contain different propensities that need to be properly balanced in a good life—reason, emotion, and appetite—is a powerful insight, however much we may want to modify the details of Plato's account.

As Plato proceeds to explore the further qualities of persons whose souls are ruled by reason, he turns to epistemology and metaphysics because the rule that reason can properly exercise requires, he supposes, exact knowledge of goodness, truth, and reality. As this account develops, we learn that those who can rule by reason must be philosophers, for whom reason and reasoning as such are the essence of human life at its best. The philosopher kings do their duty, by governing the state with the rule of reason, but what principally motivates them is not the wish to hold office but love of truth and the desire to study the unchanging realities that are only imperfectly represented in the physical world. By the end of the *Republic* the essence of the soul is taken to be pure philosophy—love of wisdom—transcending its embodied roles in ways that recall the *Phaedo*.[16]

Plato's focus on reason's guidance was not, then, confined to the political sphere. He extended it into the "life of the mind," as we use that expression when we refer to purely intellectual or aesthetic pursuits. This dimension of his philosophy is most vividly illustrated in the dialogue *Phaedrus,* where, as a winged charioteer, the soul drives a pair of winged horses, one white and the other black.[17] The charioteer stands for the soul's desire of reason. He drives his chariot high in the sky in order to travel to the place where, with "the eye of reason," he can try to observe the ultimate realities—the ideal Forms, which include the essence of the virtues. This is an image for a human being's amphibious nature, as Plotinus called it (see

POLITICIZED SOUL AND REASON

Chapter 1). We have, on the one hand, an aspiration to experience the purest form of beauty, and to transcend an earth-bound existence. But we also have a black horse in the shape of carnal desires, dragging our charioteer and our white horse down to earth. The *psyche* falls and becomes embodied in human form.

This is an amazingly bold and powerful allegory. What it shows is Plato's conviction that, to understand ourselves or our souls, we need to start from what human life can be at its best—that is to say, a life in which we identify with the desire for truth and goodness, and have the ambition (the white horse) to pursue these as goals. The body is not what we are constituted to live for. Yet, although the *psyche* is metaphysically distinct from the body, it can, and typically does, become bodily rather than spiritual in its self-identification. This occurs when reason surrenders its proper rule to *thumos* and especially to appetite, as occurs in the extreme case of the tyrant's soul. In his myths of the afterlife Plato shows what happens to souls that have failed to achieve the rule of reason. They become reincarnated in nonhuman, animal form, corresponding to the degeneracy of their souls when they lived a human life.

Because the *psyche* has a complex structure (the three parts comprising reason, *thumos,* and appetite), it manifests itself to consciousness in more than one voice, and its various voices can generate conflicting desires and a divided self. This condition, according to Plato, presents human beings with their primary task: to decide with which voice or ordering of voices they will identify themselves. Someone who identifies with appetite or with ambition, at the expense of reason and justice, is, in Plato's judgment, living a virtual animal life (recalling the image of the soul as a combination of man, lion, and many-headed beast), and hence not living the proper life of persons. The complexity of the *psyche* provides for different selves—a spectrum of self-identifications for persons, ranging from the truly philosophical right down to the fully bestial.

In the *Republic*, the soul is politicized because the question at issue is where rule should be reposed, whether the rule is external for the community or for the internal constitution of the individual soul. In the *Phaedrus*, the issue is not about politics but about how erotic desire can be sublimated and transfigured into the love of Beauty as such. Hence, the charioteer and horses model fits that dialogue in a way that would be inappropriate to the *Republic*. In the *Phaedo*, with its great drama of Socrates's final day

POLITICIZED SOUL AND REASON

on earth, Plato personifies the soul as a whole, rather than its parts, in order to make his contrast with the body as vivid as possible. For at the end of the dialogue, as Socrates's body loses its vitality under the influence of the hemlock poison, his soul departs forever from his dying frame, making it impossible, as he says, for his friends to "catch *me*."[18]

In Homer, where living human identity is psychosomatic through and through, the survivors of the dead make vain attempts to catch the phantom souls. In effect, there is nothing there for them to catch, since nothing of the real person survives death. Plato consistently reverses the Homeric model of human life. Whether or not he was completely committed to the literal immortality of individual souls, we can be sure that he had no doubts that the true essence of human beings is mental and not physiological. The tripartite model of the soul gave him a remarkable device for making this point. In life all three parts are bound together, but if immortality is possible, that will pertain only to reason. *Thumos* (spirit) and appetite, essential though they both are to our embodied life, are irreducibly mortal parts of the soul, and thus hark back to the Homeric conception. It is only reason that can equip human beings to transcend mortality, as we learn in the following memorable passage, which gives us Plato's notion of the sublime:

> Someone who is fashioned on appetites and competitive ambitions and devotes his energies to these is bound to have only mortal opinions engendered in himself.... But one devoting himself to learning and true thinking, who has trained himself in that part of himself above all is completely bound ... to have immortal and divine thoughts, if he grasps truth, and to lack no share in immortality, to the extent that this is possible for human nature; and because he is always ministering to the divine component and keeping the divine spirit itself *(daimon)* that cohabits with him well tended, he must be supremely happy *(eudaimona)*. There is only one way of ministering to anything, and that is to give it its proper nutriment and motions. The motions akin to the divine in us are the thoughts and revolutions of the universe; therefore we each need to attend to these. (*Timaeus* 90b-d)

For Plato the rule of reason has two functions. One of these is to govern the embodied soul appropriately, according to the politicized model, to ensure a socially engaged life that is harmonious for everyone. This is a practical use of reason. The other function of reason is the one expressed in the passage just quoted from the dialogue *Timaeus*. Here Plato's focus is theoretical or scientific, using reason as a guide in the pursuit of abstract truths, values, and knowledge of first principles. From what Plato says elsewhere, we can be sure that he did not think that these two functions of reason should be, or could be, kept apart from one another. The ruling guardians of the *Republic* are required to apply the fruits of their philosophical training to the practice of government and the well-being of the governed. However, they govern reluctantly, as a social duty, and not because politics is the optimal context for the exercise of reason. That is to be found by desiring knowledge for its own sake. Reason's rule in this intellectualist sense continues to carry the authoritative charge of its political and psychological functions, but here its sphere of activity is cognitive, not practical. It is a focus (startlingly novel in formulation and intensity) on the "divinity" of a life devoted to pure research.

The ancient philosopher who elaborated that project most fully was Aristotle. In concluding this chapter,

I will glance at how Aristotle drew upon and developed Plato's two functions for the rule of reason.

According to Aristotle the best and happiest life is living in accordance with "contemplative" excellence.[19] He describes this ideal as:

> the activity of intellect *(nous)* or of something else that is thought to be naturally competent to rule and to lead... whether it is divine or the most divine of the things in us. (*Nicomachean Ethics* 10.7)

The contemplative life, he continues, is the way for human beings to immortalize themselves *as far as possible*. This allusion to the passage cited from Plato's *Timaeus* is unmistakable, and so too Aristotle's calling intellect "the naturally ruling and leading faculty."

Notwithstanding his allusions to Plato, Aristotle's qualification concerning the intellect ("the divine or the most divine of the things in us") also distances him from his illustrious teacher. In a passage vividly colored by inventive personification, Plato had traced the origin of souls to a mathematical concoction designed by the divine Demiurge.[20] According to that blueprint, the soul's rationality is a literal apportionment of immortal divinity into a mortal body.

Aristotle stops short of this fancy. Rather than literal immortality, Aristotle offers the life of the contemplative mind as a virtual equivalent:

> If intellect is divine, then, in comparison with humanity, the life according to intellect is divine in comparison with human life. But we must not follow those who advise us, being human, to think of human things and, being mortal, of mortal things, but must, so far as we can, make ourselves immortal, and strain every nerve to live in accordance with the best thing in us.... And this would seem to be each human being since it is our authoritative and better part. (ibid.)

Human beings, according to some early Greek notions, were deemed to be fallen gods. Aristotle had no truck with such mythology. He verges on paradox, however, in suggesting that the best human life transcends humanity by striving to live at a divine level. Far from viewing science and theology as divergent fields, Aristotle's scientist is a quintessential theologian because the objects of contemplative study pertain to divinity's domain. In political and ethical contexts Aristotle generally deploys a bipartite division of the soul into a naturally (that is, properly) ruling element, and a naturally subordinate and nonrational component. He identifies the ruling element with intellect or thought. As for the latter component, he describes it as a combination of Plato's spirited and appetitive parts. This faculty of the soul is nonrational in the sense that it cannot think for itself or motivate the person beyond the here and now. But it can acquire a surrogate rationality by cooperating with the intellect, as in the case of someone who is temperate or brave, and it can equally resist the prescriptions of reason by prompting the person to act under the pull of immediate emotions, as in those who lack control of their appetitive desires. (*Nicomachean Ethics* 1.13)

Aristotle's rule of reason has a clear Platonic provenance, but it does not politicize the soul as directly as we observed in Plato's *Republic*. Intellect's claim to authority over the contemplative life and reason's function to guide the moral life are grounded in Aristotle's teleological conception of human nature. The soul that makes us human has many attributes. It enables our bodies to grow and reproduce and move and perceive appropriately to our natural kind, but our essential and distinctively human capacity, the basis for our life's purpose and meaning, whether we consider it in social and political life or in the context of science and pure study, is rationality.

What is so good about reason that life-long happiness and goodness depend upon its proper exercise? What has divinity to do with reason? In addition to Aristotelian notions, this book has already sketched several answers to these questions, whether we think back to Heraclitus's conformity to the world's divine rhythms (in Chapter 2), or the Socratic focus on soul as distinct from body (in Chapter 3), or Platonic aspirations to contemplate transcendent truths (as stated in this chapter). Plato and Aristotle have left us an immensely rich resource to draw upon, but they were far from exhausting Greek reflection on these huge topics. The Neoplatonist philosopher Plotinus, with whom I began Chapter 1, had his special contribution to make in the idea of the "undescended intellect," which keeps us for ever in communion with the divine. In the five centuries that separate Plotinus from his Platonic and Aristotelian predecessors, the new Hellenistic schools of Epicurus and Stoicism came to the fore. These philosophers, especially the Stoics, , as we shall now see in Chapter 5, pursued the connections between happiness, reason, and divinity in provocative ways that will make a fitting conclusion to this study of Greek models of mind and self.

Further Reading

Barnes, J., et al. (1979), eds., *Articles on Aristotle, Vol. 4: Psychology & Aesthetics* (London).

Barney, R., et al. (2012), eds., *Plato and the Divided Self* (Cambridge, UK).

Burnyeat, M. (2000), "Plato on Why Mathematics Is Good for the Soul," *Proceedings of the British Academy* 111, 1–81.

Ferrari, G. R. F (2000), ed., *Plato: The Republic.* Translated by T. Griffith (Cambridge, UK).

—— (2003), *City and Soul in Plato's Republic* (Sankt Augustin).

—— (2007), ed., *The Cambridge Companion to Plato's Republic* (Cambridge, UK).

Fine, G. (1999), ed., *Plato 2: Ethics, Politics, Religion, and the Soul* (Oxford).

Frede, D., and Reis, B. (2009), eds., *Body and Soul in Ancient Philosophy* (Berlin/New York).

Frede, M., (2011), *A Free Will: Origins of the Notion in Ancient Thought,* ed. A. A. Long (Berkeley/Los Angeles).

Hobbs, A. (2000), *Plato and the Hero: Courage, Manliness, and the Impersonal Good* (Cambridge, UK).

Long, A. A. (2011), "Aristotle on *Eudaimonia, Nous,* and Divinity" in Miller, ed., *Aristotle's Nicomachean Ethics,* 92–114.

Lorenz, H. (2006), *The Brute Within: Appetitive Desire in Plato and Aristotle* (Oxford).
Miller, J. (2011), ed., *Aristotle's Nicomachean Ethics: A Critical Guide* (Cambridge, UK).
Nightingale, A. W. (2004), *Spectacles of Truth in Classical Greek Philosophy. Theoria in its Cultural Context* (Cambridge, UK).
Price, A. W. (1995), *Mental Conflict* (London).

5

RATIONALITY, DIVINITY, HAPPINESS, AUTONOMY

PLATO CALLS THE intellectual and calculative part of the soul divine. Aristotle accords the human intellect *(nous)* a similarly exalted status. What does this ascription of divinity mean? To put the question another way, what has god, according to Greek philosophical notions of the divine, to do with reason, the government of the self, and the attainment of happiness? As modern persons, with or without religious convictions or affiliations, we are bound to be puzzled by this recourse to divinity in contexts of moral psychology. How could *any* notion of divinity help us control our passions and cultivate the life of the mind? The implications and ramifications of this question for ancient philosophy are vast. Not only Plato and Aristotle but also philosophers who came after them, most notably the Stoics, credited the human intellect with a divine pedigree and essence. Coming to terms with one's internal divinity, seeking to achieve likeness to god, perfecting one's familial and social relationships, and acquiring independence from chance or fortune—these huge notions all come together in the Stoic ethical project of living "in agreement with nature." This expression signifies a way of life and a mental disposition that fully conform to the norms of reason and, equivalently, to compliance with divinity. The other great Hellenistic school, the Garden of Epicurus, differed from Stoicism in rejecting divine creationism and divine interest in humanity. Yet Epicureans shared with Stoics the belief that divinity is the paradigm of beatitude, that a truly happy life presupposes unassailable tranquility, and that perfecting one's rationality equips human beings to become godlike as well as wise.

To investigate the theological dimension of Greek moral psychology, we need to set aside the monotheistic connotations of capitalized God as the proper name for the supreme being of Judaism, Christianity, and Islam. Greek philosophers do sometimes speak of god *(theos)* in the grammatical singular as distinct from the many gods *(theoi)* worshipped in Greek religion. Plato posits, as we have seen, a divine creator of the world, the Demiurge; Aristotle conceives of a single divine intellect, what he calls the Prime Unmoved Mover, as the world's everlasting first cause; and Stoicism draws on the hallowed name of Zeus for the unitary energizing power that shapes and pervades the world's material substance. These singular gods, however, do not exclude other divine beings from having a presence in the Platonic, or Aristotelian, or Stoic universe.[1] This combination of one and many gods should not surprise us once we reflect on the fact that the Greek philosophers were raised in the religious culture familiar to us from Homer and the tragedians in whose work there is a multitude of gods, of whom just one, Zeus, has supreme power and authority. The philosophers found the mythological features of these anthropomorphic deities incompatible with any grounds for worship and emulation, but they saw no reason to limit the extension of divinity to a single being. Instead, they regarded divinity, when purged of its unacceptable attributes and stories, as the name for the best possible type of existence, whether instantiated by one or by many beings, and distributed or distributable over a range of powers, functions, and areas.[2]

Perfection, then, was the generic conception of divinity in Greek philosophical thought, but the

RATIONALITY, DIVINITY, HAPPINESS

details of the divine life differed markedly among the main schools. Epicurus characterized his gods as "blessed and immortal beings" who live an everlastingly untroubled existence, heedless of the universe human beings inhabit.[3] Such deities, who recall the happy moments of divine jollification in Homer, provided Epicureans with their model for a sociable life that is ideally pleasurable and easygoing. In Stoicism, by contrast, the supreme divinity Zeus recalls Homer in a quite different way. Homeric Zeus, "father of gods and men," as he is often called in epic poetry, prefigures the Stoic notion of a divine mind that exercises supervisory power over the world at large. The notion of divinity in these two philosophies (and equally in the thought of Plato and Aristotle) had both a specific content distinctive of each system and also generic and shared functions. It is the latter that we need first to elaborate on, as we try to understand divinity and divine reason in Greek models of mind and care of the self.

I began Chapter 2 by drawing attention to the gap between the happiness of the immortal gods and the toils of mortal human beings. One way to close that gap, which we need not revisit here, was to extend the prospect of a blissful afterlife to deserving human souls. Attractive though that future might be, philosophers outside the Platonic tradition were not persuaded that prospects of an afterlife, supposing it to be possible, could enhance our present embodied existence; even Platonists focused their ethical thought on the soul's mental and moral improvement in life here and now. To reduce the essential gap between the divine and the human during one's ordinary lifetime, the philosophers had recourse to ideas signified by the word *eudaimonia*.

Most literally *eudaimonia* means a divinely favored dispensation. The *daimon* constituent of the word combines a generic sense of divinity with the notion of fate or fortune. By prefixing to *daimon* the adverb *eu*, which qualifies an activity or condition as excellent, the Greek language had a composite term for expressing the idea of the best possible human life, a condition of flourishing, prospering, doing extremely well. Hence *eudaimonia* is conventionally translated into English by happiness. But if happiness consists largely or entirely of material success and security, as early Greek culture had assumed, could it ever be assured? The question was especially pressing in its ancient context because the gods of mythology were notoriously quixotic and unpredictable in the ways they conferred or withdrew their favors.[4] The philosophers responded to this challenge by internalizing

RATIONALITY, DIVINITY, HAPPINESS

the chief conditions for achieving *eudaimonia*. They made "happiness" largely or entirely dependent not on external circumstances and good fortune but on persons' mental and moral dispositions. Heraclitus stated the kernel of this outlook in the following lapidary sentence: "A human being's character *(ethos)* is his fate" *(daimon)*.[5] In other words, happiness is achieved not by good luck or by what the world outside delivers but by how people shape their own destiny through their thoughts and desires and motivations.

The classic statement of this position, given the name eudaimonism by modern scholars, is put into the mouth of Socrates by Plato. This is the passage I quoted in Chapter 3, where Socrates urges the jurors at his trial to make their souls as good as possible by cultivating justice and subordinating the importance attached to bodily and external well-being. Socrates adds authority to his words by invoking throughout the defense speech his life's unswerving allegiance to divinity. In the passage I cited in Chapter 4 from Plato's *Timaeus*, a work written perhaps thirty years later, Plato exploits the etymology of the word *eudaimonia* when he attributes this condition to persons who "constantly tend their divine spirit," using the word *daimon* to refer to human beings' intellect and rational faculty, which Plato takes to be the leading constituent of their souls. Such people, according to Plato, will achieve a god-favored and flourishing life in the form of mental well-being. By cultivating their minds and subordinating the other parts of their souls to such guidance, Platonic philosophers are engaged in a form of worship—honoring their divinely given and innate powers of reason.

We can generalize Plato's fundamental point here and apply it to all the mainstream philosophical schools. By invoking divinity in their ethics and psychology, the Greek philosophers proposed that there is an essential connection between the best life that exists in the universe—namely, the divine life—and the best life that human beings can achieve or aspire to achieve. The attribution of divinity to the mind means that human beings are *naturally,* not supernaturally as we moderns might think, endowed with the capacity to live a life of unqualified excellence, happiness, and contentment. Having the capacity for living such a life does not entail, of course, that achieving this exemplary condition is probable or even practically possible for most of us. Happiness, as so construed, is an intensely demanding state of affairs because it requires human beings not only to cultivate their rationality but also to prioritize it above everything else, especially one's instinctual wants and short-term bodily satisfactions. Nonetheless, the divinity of happiness marked it out as the supremely excellent aspiration. It also elevated human dignity to the highest extent possible in contrast with the lowly status of mortals that is characteristically voiced in Homeric epic.

I have just used the expression "powers of reason." This is a notion closely akin to the notion of the "rule of reason," which we studied in Chapter 4. As we investigate the genealogy of the philosophers' theological psychology, the notion of power (*dynamis*) demands particular attention. Divinity in every culture is understood to be the source of exceptionally powerful agency. Gods are traditionally and basically taken to be beings that make very big things happen, things that fundamentally matter to us for good or for ill, such as storms or fine weather. Power goes along with causality. Are reason and rationality, we may wonder, powers in the sense of being causally efficacious, so as to make things happen? The answer, according to the Greek philosophers, is unequivocally affirmative, provided that we understand power in a way that combines force and energy with teleology and organizational effectiveness. It is this special sense of causal power that is at work in the goodness and purposiveness of reason and that makes reason divine.

What I am saying in these rather abstract ways is expressed most memorably and concretely in Plato's description of the motivations and activities of the divine Demiurge, who is his figurative expression for the world's creative agent.[6] We are to take this creator deity to be a supremely generous applied mathematician. The Demiurge manifests these qualities by imposing geometrical structure and orderly motion on a preexisting physical chaos. If Plato had been writing in the seventeenth century, he could have said that his divine creator drafted the Laws of Nature. Plato attributes the Demiurge's cosmological acts to his excellence, manifested in his wanting "everything to be good and nothing bad, as far as this was attainable," and so akin to himself.[7] The Demiurge "generated order out of disorder, considering that order was in every way preferable." An essential component of this creative and organizing act was the introduction of intelligence into the newly ordered world. The Demiurge achieves that result by creating a rational soul for the world itself (active most evidently in the harmony of celestial motions) and also by creating the particular intelligent souls that become embodied in human beings.

RATIONALITY, DIVINITY, HAPPINESS

Plato calls his account of divine creation a "likely [or reasonable] story." That phrase means that we are not to take the details, especially the personalized Demiurge, as exactly literal truths. I draw on the passage because it enables us to see why Greek philosophers could consider reason not simply as the mental instrument for effective planning or calculating but as a supreme living being in its own right, indeed as the very essence of goodness by virtue of its power to generate and maintain order, structure, and harmony.

Among the earliest Greek cosmologists who offered theories about the origin of the world, the one who anticipated Plato most directly was Anaxagoras, a contemporary of Socrates and the author of the first philosophical best seller.[8] Anaxagoras originated a distinction between mind *(nous)* and matter, taking matter to be inert and undifferentiated stuff, and mind to be the quite separate and distinct entity that generates the cosmos. This cosmic intellect activates and sifts the primordial material mass, causing it to form into the elementary substances of the physical world. The surviving words of Anaxagoras do not explicitly attribute goodness or purposiveness or even divinity to his cosmic mind (though he writes of it in august language), but we should take all these attributes to be implicit in his looking to *nous* as the world's generative power. The basic sense of that word is precisely intelligence and foresight. Anaxagoras, who earned the nickname Mind on account of his theory, posited a superhuman intellect as the power required to make sense of the orderly universe that we inhabit and observe.

Modeling the mind, as we saw in Chapter 4, could draw heavily upon political notions of rule(r) and subordinate(s) or on the social distinction between master and slave. What we are now seeing, with the present focus on cosmology, is a notion of reason or mind or mathematical intelligence as the source of the physical world's order and structure. That postulate is a huge idea, especially when we compare it with mythological accounts of divine rule, including even the "far-seeing mind" of Olympian Zeus. I am not stating the truism that human beings need reason in order to bring the world within the scope of scientific understanding. My point is rather the proposition that physics is possible only because the world itself is the product of reason as manifested in the activity and effect of divine purpose and divine intelligence.

This argument from design took different forms in different schools. In Plato and Stoicism, most directly, the world owes its generation to the providential craftsmanship of a superhuman intelligence. Aristotle also makes divine intellect the world's first cause, but less directly. Rather than being a providential creator, the Prime Mover is a thinker whose excellence is reflected and transmitted throughout the purposiveness of all natural events, especially the structure and functions of living beings. The essence of Aristotelian happiness, whether we view it in the contemplative sphere (orderly thinking about theoretical topics) or in social life (deliberating how best to organize our desires in conformity with the practical virtues), is the excellent activity of our soul's rational faculty. And reason for Aristotle is both essentially good and essentially divine. As he states most memorably in the context of describing the life of the Prime Unmoved Mover, human thinking at its momentary best is like the divine mind's everlasting activity.[9]

Epicureans, for whom the world's first principle is matter in motion, had no use for a divine mind as a causal and creative principle in physics. Hence they unequivocally rejected the argument from design. They agreed, however, that reason is a power, or rather *the* power, by which human beings can generate orderly, tranquil, and virtuous lives.[10] As for the

Epicurean gods, these mysterious beings signify the ideal life for human beings to emulate. They are presumably wise, because without wisdom it would not be possible for them to negotiate appropriate sources of pleasure or avoid falling victim to desires the fulfillment of which is neither natural nor necessary for happiness. Moreover, as Cicero says on behalf of Epicurean philosophy, divine happiness requires that gods be both virtuous and rational.[11]

Thus far I have been discussing the generic conception of reason, with a view to showing why the leading Greek thinkers viewed it as a divine attribute, and invoked it as the most potent source of human well-being. Underlying this linkage between happiness, reason, and divinity are three propositions: first, that divine lives are systematically excellent in virtue of their rationality; second, that human beings have the mental equipment to emulate divine excellence; and third, that the human equivalent to divine excellence is happiness, construed as an untroubled and rationally guided mentality. I turn now, and for the remainder of this chapter, to the ideas on these matters developed by the Stoic philosophers.

Like Plato, Aristotle, and Epicurus, the Stoics grounded human excellence and happiness in a way of life consistently guided by reason. Again like these predecessors, they regarded reason and its guidance as attributes of divinity. But Stoic divinity does not transcend the physical world, as it does in these other philosophies. The Stoic Zeus is a pantheistic deity, internal to the universe, who generates the physical world from inside by pervading and giving form to matter.[12] In its providential and creative activity, the Stoic Zeus closely resembles the Platonic Demiurge. The main difference is that Plato's divine craftsman does not get his hands dirty, as it were, whereas the Stoics' counterpart is taken to be a physical force as well as a mind. Every natural substance or body in the Stoic universe has divinity present to it as its causal principle. Because the acts of Zeus are rational, everything conforms to reason from the divine perspective, whether we refer to the motions of the heavens, the structure of minerals, the principles of botanical and zoological phenomena, or the physical and mental attributes of human beings.

This all-encompassing divinity is also called nature and cause in Stoic theory.

> Since universal nature reaches everywhere, it must be the case that however anything happens in the whole and in any of its parts it

> happens in accordance with universal nature
> and *its reasons* in unhindered sequence. This is
> because there is nothing that could interfere
> with nature's government from outside, nor is
> there any way for any of the parts to enter any
> process or state except in accordance with
> universal nature.[13]

What we have in this account, composed by the early Stoic philosopher Chrysippus, is a notion of the world as a completely closed and determinate system. Yet, rather than that notion's furnishing, as we might suppose that it would, the model of a purely mechanistic and lifeless universe, the Stoic philosophers take the cosmos to be pulsating with intelligence, with the result that whatever happens occurs *for reasons,* and moreover for the best of reasons. Occurring for reasons, just as in Platonism and Aristotle, does not mean only that rational minds can attempt to understand why natural events occur as they are seen to do; it means in addition, and much more importantly in ethical and psychological contexts, that rational minds are equipped to understand and appreciate the world from the world's point of view. To put it another way, Stoicism maintains that human beings are capable of adopting a decentered or objective perspective on natural events, including those events that impinge directly on us and on what we hold most dear. We achieve this perspective ("living in agreement with human *and* universal nature") by acknowledging that nothing that falls outside human agency could be different from what actually happens or better than what actually happens. Natural events outside the human sphere are divinity's business—for instance, the changes of the seasons, the sun's rising and setting, the mortality of terrestrial life forms, our genetic makeup, and even disasters such as earthquakes and tsunamis. These things are to be accepted and responded to with the understanding that they are how things had to be, in the physical world that the divine intellect has constituted and brought to pass.

This position, without further explanation, might seem to warrant fatalism or at least greatly diminish the significance of human agency. Actually, however, it has the opposite import. This is because the deterministic structure of divine causality and external events, far from excluding human autonomy and responsibility, makes special room for them through the Stoic doctrine that our minds are "parts" or "offshoots" of the divine intellect. In the Stoic universe, agency (meaning the causality specific to minds) is distributed between the supreme intellect of Zeus or universal nature, which is the absolute divine, and the derivative rationality of persons. The power of the former is immeasurable, but thanks to the latter persons can in principle adapt appropriately to everything that impinges directly on their lives. This bold doctrine assigns human beings the capacity to become completely autonomous, meaning subject to no authority beyond the rule of reason. That rule is both subjective and objective because it presupposes partnership between the individual self and the absolute divine.

To set the Stoic scene further I draw on a selection of passages from the philosopher Epictetus (ca. CE 55–135), which he composed as lectures for his Roman students. The common theme of these passages is the rational nature of the human mind and its relation or potential relation to divinity. Epictetus likes to apply personalist language in his accounts of the school's cosmic divinity, rather than calling it universal nature, as Chrysippus had done. He expresses the implications of providential pantheism for humanity and for the human mind in a discourse that I will quote at length, numbering its sections for convenience.

RATIONALITY, DIVINITY, HAPPINESS

(1.1) If plants and our own bodies are so connected and interactive with the universe, does that not apply all the more to our minds? And if our minds are so connected and attached to god, as parts and offshoots of his being, does god not perceive their every movement as something belonging to him and sharing in his nature? (1.2) You, for your part, have the capacity to reflect on the divine government and each one of its features, and similarly on human affairs; and you have the capacity to be moved by countless things simultaneously, *in your senses and your thinking, assenting to or rejecting some of them, and suspending judgment about others. In your mind you retain so many impressions from such a great range of things, and under their influence you find yourself having ideas corresponding to your initial impressions, and from countless things you secure a series of skills and memories.*[14] (1.3) Is god, then, not capable of overseeing everything and being present with everything and maintaining a certain distribution with everything? ... He has presented to each person each person's own divine spirit *(daimon)*, as a guardian, and

committed the person's safekeeping to this
trustee, who does not sleep and who cannot be
misled. To what better and more caring
guardian could he have entrusted us? (1.4) So
when you close your doors and make it dark
inside, remember never to say you are alone,
because you are not. God is inside and your
own divine spirit, too.... It is to this god that
you should swear allegiance, as soldiers do to
Caesar.... (1.5) What, then, will you swear?
Never to disobey, or press charges, or complain
about anything god has given you, or be
reluctant in doing or suffering anything that is
inevitable. Is this oath anything like that other
one? There men swear to put no one ahead of
Caesar. But here we swear to put ourselves
ahead of everything else.[15]

There are echoes here of familiar monotheistic
doctrines, especially the presumption that human
beings are God's special charge, that they are made
in God's image, and that God is omniscient, providential, and beyond reproach. But the great doctrinal texts of those religions are largely silent on God's
rationality. Moreover, it would be impious for a traditional Christian or Jew or Muslim to presume that

RATIONALITY, DIVINITY, HAPPINESS

God's mind or God's thoughts are directly accessible to human beings. In Stoicism by contrast, the mind of Zeus is taken to have the same basic faculties (more on these below) that a perfected human intellect has, but to have them to an exponentially more powerful degree. Epictetus embellishes this point (sections 1.1–1.2) by using our own minds as evidence of, and actually as proof for, the immensity of the principal Stoic god's powers of thought and discernment. Zeus is both the cause of and the reason why natural and biological phenomena conform to an orderly structure. We can see divine rationality consummately at work in the world's rhythms and regular changes. Stoicism is completely at one with Plato and Aristotle on this cosmology.

Epictetus now makes an extraordinary shift from this external, visible context to an internal, invisible, and intensely personal perspective. The author of the universe, we are to infer, is actually within us as well as being outside us (1.3). Zeus's powers extend to, and even extend into, each person's particular mind. They bear upon us, not in the sense of forming one's momentary consciousness, but as constituting one's capacity to feel at home in the universe ("not alone") even under adverse circumstances, and to dispose oneself accordingly.

Epictetus expresses this interaction between the divine and the human by calling the mind "a divine spirit" *(daimon)*. The scope of this ancient word, as we have seen, extends from divinity in general to fate or fortune, as evident in the word *eudaimonia*. Plato and Aristotle had anticipated Epictetus's usage to some extent (see Chapter 4), but they did not envision the human mind and its rationality as a direct offshoot of god by making it an integral part of the world's reason. This Stoic doctrine gives human beings a special status in the universe, both in their direct "kinship" as rational beings with Zeus, and in their interpersonal relationships to other people or other "divine spirits."[16] The doctrine also sets human beings their primary task—to align their individual share of reason and appropriate action with its universal source. In concrete terms, this task involves making the best (most reasonable and admirable) use of all situations and environments that are beyond one's own power to create or to change.

To understand what the Stoics mean by reason is also to understand their technical analysis of the mind and the self. Epictetus treats this huge topic compendiously in his first, programmatic discourse. He starts out with a disquisition on the uniqueness, in the set of all skills and faculties, of what he calls

RATIONALITY, DIVINITY, HAPPINESS

"the reasoning power" (*logike dynamis*, *Discourse* I.1.4), which is equivalent to "divine spirit." No other faculty, he says, is able to study itself as well as everything else.[17] The scope of the reasoning faculty covers what we would call both facts and values. That is to say, this faculty is our means not only of understanding and identifying things, and discriminating between truth and falsehood, but also of assigning significance and worth to things. That last function includes especially our experience of how the world impinges upon us through our senses and what we decide to make of that experience.

Epictetus turns again to theology in order to draw a contrast between the reasoning power, as so described, and the body and all bodily attributes. Divinity, in its creative benevolence, has done the best it could do for human beings. Creatures consisting of flesh, bones, and blood cannot but be limited in what they are able to do as embodied beings. Our bodies could not have been made invulnerable and still be bodies, nor could any embodied being have complete control over its limbs and organs in every conceivable circumstance. The mind too, according to Stoic doctrine, is a physical structure, unlike the incorporeal soul of Platonism. Yet, nothing in the world can prevent the mind, according to Epictetus, from assenting to what is true, dissenting from what is false, and suspending judgment on what it finds uncertain (*Discourse* 1.17.21-3).

Epictetus imagines the following conversation between himself and Zeus, with Zeus speaking as follows:

> If it had been possible, I would have made your little body and property free and unhindered. But in fact—take note of my words—this is not your own but only artfully molded clay. Since I could not give you this, I have given you a portion of myself, this faculty of positive and negative volition and of desire and aversion—the faculty, in short, of using mental impressions. By caring for this and by situating all that is yours therein, you will never be impeded, you will never be restricted, you will not groan or find fault or flatter anyone. (*Discourse* 1.1.10-12)

As is his wont, Epictetus combines psychology with ethics. The purpose of his doing so, and indeed of his focus on the reasoning faculty, is to give his students a sense of their essential identity as human beings—identity in the sense of both their common humanity and their particular selfhood. Drawing again on his own words, I quote four further passages:

RATIONALITY, DIVINITY, HAPPINESS

> God has entrusted me to myself, and he has subordinated my volition to me alone, giving me standards for its correct use. (*Discourse* 4.12.12)

> God has committed yourself to you, and he says: "I had no one more trustworthy than you; keep this person for me in the way that is his nature, reverent, trustworthy, upright, undismayed, unimpassioned, undisturbed." (*Discourse* 2.8.23)

> Study who you are. First of all, a human being—that is, one who has nothing more authoritative than volition, but who holds everything else subordinate to that while keeping it free and sovereign. Consider, next, from what creatures you are separated by possessing reason. You are separated from wild beasts, you are separated from sheep. (*Discourse* 2.10.1–2)

> You are not flesh or hair but volition; if you keep that beautiful, you will be beautiful. (*Discourse* 3.1.40)

Epictetus posits an integral connection between reason, the self, and volition, which is my translation of his Greek term *prohairesis*. He also, as we have seen, glosses his analysis of "the reasoning power" by asserting that we have a god-given faculty of how to "use our mental impressions." To get as clear as possible about the Stoic model of mind underlying these notions, we should step back for a moment to the Stoics' main predecessors.

Modeling the mind in ancient philosophy could take the form of partitioning it into distinct "parts." We have witnessed that procedure in the case of Plato and Aristotle. Both of these philosophers drew attention to desires of reason, on the one hand, and impulses that they termed nonrational *(alogoi)* on the other hand. The existence of such impulses seemed to them (as it may also seem to us) to be an obvious consequence and requirement of our embodied nature, aligning us, in our needs for food, rest, and the company of our kind, with animal life in general. Desires of reason, by contrast, differentiated us from the rest of the animal world, from which the divine essence or nature was totally absent. Divinity did not pertain to the mind in its entirety but only to its higher and uniquely human aspect, making control of nonrational, animal-like impulses one of the mind's most important functions in living a good life.

RATIONALITY, DIVINITY, HAPPINESS

Stoic philosophers rejected this partitioning of the mind into rational and nonrational parts. They recognized that human beings often behave irrationally under the influence of strong emotions, which they took to be faulty judgments. They did not deny that people often act in bestial ways. But they took such behavior to be a misuse of reason. They sharply distinguished such irrationality (thoughtless or stupid or antisocial actions) from the nonrational behavior of other animals. Only a rational being, they argued, can behave irrationally, meaning act contrary to the dictates of sound reasoning. According to the Stoic model, the human mind consists of several faculties, but these faculties are all functions of reason, making the mind (sometimes called "the commanding faculty of the soul") a unity, unlike its Platonic and Aristotelian counterpart.

The Stoics acknowledged of course that human beings are a species of animal, and that this generic nature extends not only to bodily properties but also to certain mental attributes. The latter include the abilities to process sensory information *(phantasia)* and to respond to that data by the motivation *(horme)* to behave appropriately to the environment. In the case of nonhuman animals, this input/output or stimulus/response causality was taken to be instinctual in the sense that such creatures are born fully equipped to live in their specific ways. Interestingly, though, the Stoics described that instinctual ability, even in non-human animals, as "self-perception."

How, we should then ask, did the Stoics envision the mentality of human infants? The answer they gave is that human infants are "not yet rational" because reason requires extensive time and experience to develop. According to the Stoic view, we begin our mental lives just like other animals, by processing sensory data and responding to it in appropriate ways. However, in addition to the generic mental faculties of impression or consciousness *(phantasia)* and motivation or drive *(horme)*, human beings are naturally endowed with a third faculty, which (following Cicero's Latin terminology) is generally rendered into English by the term "assent." Human infants have the rudimentary self that other animals perceive from the moment of birth, but in addition, thanks to their faculty of "assent," they also have the potentiality to become a fully rational self, by which the Stoics mean the ability to become reflective and autonomous persons. With the completion of that process human beings are equipped to achieve their normative identity as divine spirits.

RATIONALITY, DIVINITY, HAPPINESS

We have already encountered the term *assent* in contexts from Epictetus. To elucidate its range and function in Stoic moral psychology, let us also recall his use of the terms *self-study, volition, sovereign,* and *ability to use impressions.* Epictetus was teaching four hundred and more years after Zeno founded the Stoic school at Athens in about 300 BCE. I mention this history because it was Zeno himself who made assent the most distinctive and original contribution to the Stoic model of mind and self.

We don't possess Zeno's own account of the doctrine, but the Greek word that he used for it was a noun that he almost certainly coined, *synkatathesis*. This word is derived from a verb, the basic meaning of which is to put down one's vote for something, to endorse an opinion, to align oneself with (the word's prefix means "with"), or to accept the truth of a proposition. Hence we find the verb assigned to Socrates by Plato in a context where Socrates asks his interlocutor whether he shares or opposes Socrates's judgment.[18] Zeno and his Stoic followers presented themselves as devotees of Socrates. I conjecture that Zeno took himself to have strong Socratic authority for positing his original concept of the mind's faculty of assent. Nothing that Socrates said was better known or more challenging than his insistence on the "uselessness of the unexamined life" or the folly of mistaking one's own ignorance for knowledge.[19] Socrates, according to Plato, claimed divine authority for this injunction. Thus we may imagine that Zeno already regarded assent as a god-given faculty, just as Epictetus did.

Here is how Cicero describes Zeno's innovation in highly summary fashion:

> Zeno made some novel statements about sense perceptions. He regarded them as compounded out of an impact presented from outside (which he called *phantasia* . . .). To these sense impressions he adjoined the mind's assent, which he took to be located within us and voluntary.[20]

The critical word in this compressed passage is *voluntary,* meaning "up to us" or "dependent on our will" or "free from external constraint." As I said previously, Stoics explained the behavior of nonhuman animals and that of human infants by means of an input/output or stimulus/response model. Thus, for instance, a spider has the sense impression *(phantasia)* that its web has caught a fly; it responds to that impression by launching itself *(horme)* to devour its prey. These two faculties, sense perception and impulse, in concert with the spider's arachnid nature, are sufficient to account for the spider's behavior. The creature does not need to weigh, interpret, and evaluate its visual experience in any cognitively elaborate way. To put it in Stoic terms, a spider has no need for volition or assent in the form of a capacity to make decisions concerning the impulses it receives from its sense impressions.

This is precisely what Zeno introduced with his theory of assent. Like all animals we are constantly presented with sensory information. We are also, to a much greater extent presumably than other creatures, constantly subject to internally generated thoughts and representations. What we experience through our senses depends on the state of the external world and how we position ourselves. We have only limited control over whatever else comes into our heads moment by moment. Such experience, much of it inevitably tinged with likes and dislikes, colors our consciousness, making us recipients rather than agents. This passivity, however, is precisely what the faculty of assent limits, modifies, and transforms. Sense impressions and other kinds of representations are triggers of action and emotion, but only if and when we assent to them. There is no necessary or automatic connection between having the sense impression or thought of an attractive object, and actually desiring and pursuing the object. Correspondingly, impressions or thoughts of painful or unattractive states of affairs trigger negative reactions or avoidance only if and when we accept or decide that something really bad for us is in the offing.

Zeno's point was not, or not primarily, that human actions are governed by what people choose or wish or desire to do. That proposition is self-evident. You can believe it irrespective of whether you think human beings are capable of genuine self-determination. My reading of Zeno's voluntarism is that he made autonomous assent, which we can also call the will or the ego or volition or personhood (the names do not matter), the center of agency. According to this view, human history is not reducible to a congeries of social forces, external to individuals, but to what individual persons make of themselves. The doctrine of autonomous assent has often been found difficult to accommodate to the strict causal nexus that links all events in the Stoic universe.[21] Actually, however, the causal nexus would be hopelessly broken and interrupted without the activity and the gift of assent. How, otherwise, could it be the case that what was done, as it *was* done, was precisely and only your act or my act? Human beings would not be integral

RATIONALITY, DIVINITY, HAPPINESS

"parts" of divine causality, as they are presumed to be, unless they were equally presumed to be agents in their own right. Moreover, independently of Stoicism, the specifics of agency require that the human mind have a faculty of assent or something like it. And this holds true, in the way we experience and know ourselves, irrespective of any biochemical facts about the brain.

We can now see why Epictetus frequently characterizes appropriate behavior with the expression "making correct use of impressions." Underlying this notion is a vast array of Stoic ethical doctrine concerning things that are truly good or bad for human beings and society, the conditions for happiness, the reasons for unhappiness, and much more that we need not explore here. Epictetus captures the central point in a context where he is advising a student on how to modify bad habits and addictions and resist initially alluring impressions:

> Adopt the wish to please yourself, wish to make yourself beautiful in the sight of god. Resolve to make yourself clean in company with your clean self and with god.... In this way you will defeat the impression *(phantasia)* and not be dragged off by it. Start by not being smitten by

its intensity, but say: "Wait for me a little,
O Impression. Let me see who you are and what
you are about, let me test you." And next, do
not let it lead you on by picturing the sequel.
Otherwise, it will be off and take you wherever
it wants. Instead, conjure up a different and a
fair impression, and banish this foul one.
(*Discourse* 2.18.19–25)

This passage, composed in Epictetus's characteristically homey style, brilliantly conveys the centrality of assent to the Stoic model of mind. It also evokes Epictetus's admonitions concerning divinity's presence within the self. Let us also recall his earlier words about the mind's capacity to monitor desires and aversions. In that passage Epictetus describes this capacity as the essence of reason, heralded as the divine gift that equips human beings to take total command of themselves and their experience.

The voluntarism that Zeno credited to assent underlies this Stoic doctrine. We can control our external situation and even our bodies only to a limited extent. What escapes this limitation, at least in principle, is assent, or in more familiar language, one's will or decision making or one's character. As human individuals, each of us has a life that only you or only I can live. We live that life for good or ill by how we deploy our mental resources, by the use we make of our impressions, and by the responsibility we take for our actions. Here, if I am not mistaken, there is no gap between the Stoic model of mind and our own phenomenological experience.

In order to dramatize the mind's potential autonomy, Stoic teachers liked to present their students with exceptionally striking examples, such as Socrates's unflinching response to an unjust death sentence or the Roman Cato's suicide as a decision for liberty in the face of tyranny. But these rhetorical gestures may be set aside here. Most of us are not called upon to be heroic. More than other ancient philosophers, the Stoics were highly sensitive to human beings' uncontrollable reactions and to individual differences of aptitude and temperament. Their focus on assent and volition makes no presupposition about what persons *should* do. It is an invitation, rather, to enlarge the range of one's options, self-assessments, and performance expectations. We may also view it as a salutary antidote to media pressures and the measurement of happiness by external outcomes. The divinity of reason and our share of that divinity may be a helpful trope even for a thoroughly secular world. What it points to, in the final analysis, at least for us, is not an outmoded theology but a luminous metaphor for our shared humanity and for the potential dignity of each human spirit.

Further Reading

Bobzien, S. (1998), *Determinism and Freedom in Stoic Philosophy* (Oxford).

Cooper, J. (1999), *Reason and Emotion: Essays on Ancient Moral Psychology and Ethical Theory* (Princeton), especially chapter 20.

Gerson, L. P. (1990), *God and Greek Philosophy: Studies in the Early History of Natural Theology* (London/New York).

Graver, M. (2003), "Not Even Zeus: A Discussion of A. A. Long, Epictetus: A Stoic and Socratic Guide to Life," *Oxford Studies in Ancient Philosophy* 25, 345–62.

Inwood, B. (1985), *Ethics and Human Action in Early Stoicism* (Oxford).

Long, A. A. (1986), *Hellenistic Philosophy: Stoics, Epicureans, Sceptics,* 2nd ed. (Berkeley/Los Angeles).

—— (2002), *Epictetus: A Stoic and Socratic Guide to Life* (Oxford), especially chapters 6 and 8.

—— (2004), "Eudaimonism, Divinity, and Rationality in Greek Ethics," in *Proceedings of the Boston Area Colloquium in Ancient Philosophy,* vol. 19 (2003), ed. J. J. Cleary and G. M. Gurtler (Leiden/Boston), 123–44.

Nightingale, A., and Sedley, D. (2010), eds., *Ancient Models of Mind: Studies in Human and Divine Rationality* (Cambridge).

Reydams-Schils, G. (2005), *The Roman Stoics: Self, Responsibility, and Affection* (Chicago).

—— (2010), "Seneca's Platonism: The Soul and Its Divine Origin," in Nightingale/Sedley, *Ancient Models of Mind*, 196–215.

Sedley, D. (2007), *Creationism and Its Critics in Antiquity* (Berkeley/Los Angeles), especially chapters 4 and 7.

Silverman, A. (2010), "Contemplating Divine Mind," in Nightingale/Sedley, *Ancient Models of Mind*, 75–96.

EPILOGUE

In this book I have discussed a range of models of self in Greek literature and thought, starting with Homer and moving forward in time to Stoicism. Over the course of these centuries, we have seen many different ideas and questions unfold about human identity. Are human beings essentially mortal, as the Homeric epics emphatically assume, or do we have the possibility of achieving immortality, as Plato frequently maintains? When and why do explicit ideas about the differences between body and soul start to emerge? Does the mind have a complex structure? What gave rise to the notion that the best life is a life ruled by reason, with desires and emotions subordinated to that rule? What did it mean to think of the human intellect as a divine faculty?

Homer's great figures are brilliantly vivid in their energy and passion. We recognize many aspects of

EPILOGUE

our selves in their thoughts and feelings. But Homer's characters register only a fraction of human potential. At another extreme, we may recall the Platonists' lovers of reason, subjugating their appetites and worldly ambitions in order to focus upon the timeless truths of perfect being. There, too, we encounter human potential, but only a fraction of it again. How could that be otherwise? How could any account of the mind encompass everything about us?

The Stoic tradition is strongly Socratic and Platonic in its focus on the rule of reason and the indifference of material success for the human good. But Stoic philosophers were this-worldly in their rejection of Plato's supra-sensible Forms and the immortality of the soul. Rather than flirting with utopianism or reformist aspirations, the thinkers of this school focused attention on making the best possible use of one's immediate material circumstances, in whatever time and place and station persons find themselves to be situated. What Stoicism chiefly contributes to human potential is the idea of a mind in which autonomy, rationality, self-worth, integrity, and philanthropy can be fully integrated with one another. Here is the way Marcus Aurelius, Emperor of Rome (161–180 CE), formulated this prescription

GREEK MODELS OF MIND AND SELF

in the Epictetus-influenced *Meditations* that he addressed to himself. In light of my discussion in the preceding pages, and especially my citations from Epictetus, no further commentary is needed.

> Never value as beneficial to yourself something that will force you one day to break your word, abandon your integrity, hate, suspect, or curse someone else, pretend, or desire something that needs the secrecy of walls or curtains. The one who has chosen to value above all *his own mind and divine spirit* and the worship of its excellence does not make a drama of his life or complain and will not need either isolation or crowds of people; most of all, he will live neither pursuing nor avoiding things. He does not care in any way whether he will have his soul enclosed by his body for a longer or shorter time. Even if he needs to leave right away, he departs as readily as if he were performing any of the other actions that can be done in a decent and orderly way, exercising care for this alone throughout his life, that *his mind should never be in a state that is alien to that of a rational and social being.*[1]

ANCIENT AUTHORS AND THINKERS

NOTES

INDEX

ANCIENT AUTHORS AND THINKERS

Anaxagoras (c. 500-427 BCE): Greek philosopher from Ionia, who spent time in Athens and probably knew Socrates there. His work is translated in R. McKirahan, *Philosophy before Socrates: An Introduction with Texts and Commentary,* 2nd ed. (Indianapolis, 2010).

Aristotle (384-322 BCE): Macedonian student in Plato's Academy, and founder of the Peripatetic school of philosophy at Athens. His works are translated in J. Barnes, ed., *The Complete Works of Aristotle: The Revised Oxford Translation,* 2 vols. (Princeton, 1984).

Aurelius, Marcus (CE 121-80): Roman Emperor and author of *Meditations;* see C. Gill, *Marcus Aurelius: Meditations, Books 1-6* (Oxford, 2013).

Chrysippus (c. 280-206 BCE): Leading Stoic philosopher from Asia Minor, who immigrated to Athens. Translations of his fragmentary works are excerpted in LS *Hellenistic Philosophers*.

ANCIENT AUTHORS AND THINKERS

Cicero (106–43 BCE): Roman orator, statesman, and philosopher.

Empedocles (c. 495–435 BCE): Greek philosopher from Agrigento in Sicily. His work is translated in McKirahan (2010).

Epictetus (c. CE 55–135): Stoic philosopher and educator, born in Asia Minor. He spent his early life as a slave in Rome, and later years as a freedman teaching in Greece. His works are translated in full by R. Hard in C. Gill, ed., *The Discourses of Epictetus* (London, 1995), and selectively by A. A. Long in *Epictetus: A Stoic and Socratic Guide to Life* (Oxford, 2002).

Epicurus (341–271 BCE): Athenian founder of the Garden School of philosophy. Translations of his fragmentary works are excerpted in LS *Hellenistic Philosophers*.

Gorgias (c. 484–376 BCE): Rhetorician and sophist from Sicily. His work is translated in McKirahan (2010), and in M. Gagarin and P. Woodruff, eds., *Early Greek Political Thought from Homer to the Sophists* (Cambridge, 1995).

Heraclitus (b. c. 530 BCE): Greek philosopher from Ephesus. His work is translated in C. H. Kahn, *The Art and Thought of Heraclitus: A New Arrangement and Translation of the Fragments with Literary and Philosophical Commentary* (Cambridge, UK, 1979), and in McKirahan (2010).

ANCIENT AUTHORS AND THINKERS

Herodotus (c. 484–420 BCE): Greek historian from Asia Minor.

Hesiod (c. 700 BCE): Greek poet. There are good translations of his *Works and Days* and *Theogony* by M. L. West (Oxford, 1983) and S. Lombardo (Indianapolis, 1993).

Homer (c. 700 BCE): Reputed author of *Iliad* and *Odyssey*. There are good translations by R. Lattimore, R. Fagles, and S. Lombardo.

Isocrates (436–338 BCE): Athenian orator and political theorist. His works are translated by G. Norlin (Cambridge, MA, 1928).

Lucretius (c. 94–55 BCE): Roman poet and Epicurean philosopher. His work is translated by R. Latham, rev. J. Godwin (London, 1954).

Pindar (518–438 BCE): Greek lyric poet. His works are translated by A. Verity (Oxford, 2007).

Plato (427–347 BCE): Athenian philosopher. The standard translation is J. Cooper, ed., *Plato: Complete Works* (Indianapolis, 1997).

Plotinus (CE 205–270): Platonist philosopher, probably born in Egypt. His *Enneads* are most accessible in the free translation by S. MacKenna, ed. J. Dillon (London, 1991).

Protagoras (mid fifth century BCE): Greek sophist; see Gagarin and Woodruff (1995).

Pyrrho (c. 365–270 BCE): Greek originator of the philosophical movement later called Skepticism; see *LS Hellenistic Philosophers*.

Pythagoras (b. c. 535 BCE): Greek religious leader who emigrated from Samos in Ionia to southern Italy and founded a cult there; see McKirahan (2010).

Socrates (470–399 BCE): Athenian philosopher extensively portrayed in Plato's dialogues.

Sophocles (c. 496–306 BCE): Athenian tragedian.

Thucydides (c. 455–400 BCE): Athenian historian.

Zeno (334–262 BCE): Cypriot founder of Stoic school of philosophy at Athens; see *LS Hellenistic Philosophers*.

NOTES

Introduction

1. *Die Philosophie der Griechen in ihrer Geschichtlichen Entwicklung.* The work passed through many editions between 1844 and 1902. An eloquent denunciation of "the progressivist view" is made by Bernard Williams in the first chapter of his book *Shame and Necessity*.
2. We have retained the cardiovascular "model" for many English language contexts. Just note our many words formed from *heart* to express feeling or energizing (*heartfelt, hearten, whole-hearted, heartsick, heartstrings, heartbreak*), with no comparable terms formed from *brain*. *Brainy* and *brainless* are interestingly different from *hearty* and *heartless,* with intelligence or its lack as the focus of the former. And *heartache,* as we all know, is a condition registered by the brain, but we don't call it a *headache*. The heart is where we

experience feeling, and that is enough for our self-understanding, or at least for how we talk about our condition. Anatomical truths do not and probably cannot keep pace with subjective experience.

CHAPTER 1 *Psychosomatic Identity*

1. *Ennead* 1.6. The exact title of this work is "What Is the Living Being and What Is the Human Being?"
2. *Psychai* is the plural form of *psyche*.
3. *Odyssey* 11.74.
4. Because Plutarch was a voluminous author, several works were misattributed to him in later antiquity. This work, most commonly entitled *On the Life and Poetry of Homer*, has been edited and translated by J. J. Keaney and R. Lamberton (Atlanta, 1996).
5. See sections 120 and 127 of Keaney/Lamberton.
6. Diogenes Laertius, *Lives of Eminent Philosophers* 9.67.
7. The etymology of *psyche* is not certain, but the word is probably derived from a root that signifies *breathe,* as ancient Greek usage itself suggests. Homer does not attribute *psyche* or *soma* to his immortal gods, thereby confirming the connection of these words with mortality. By contrast, he regularly credits the gods as well as human beings with his favorite "psychological"

terms *thumos*, *phrenes*, and *noos*. In Hesiod, Homer's near contemporary poet (see Chapter 2), *psyche* can signify "life" in the sense of one's vital possession (*Works and Days* 686), and *soma* can refer to a living body (ibid. 540).

8. Aristotle discusses the character of the type of person he calls *megalopsycho in Nicomachean Ethics* 4.3.

9. Snell published his work under the title *Die Entdeckung des Geistes. Studien zur Entstehung des europäischen Denkens bei den Griechen* (first German edition, Göttingen, 1946). It is best known through the English translation by T. G. Rosenmeyer, entitled *The Discovery of the Mind. The Greek Origins of European Thought* (Oxford, 1953). Williams 2008 (originally 1993) criticizes Snell at length. I discuss his critique in Long 2007.

10. Plato, *Republic* 4, 440b, 411a, 8, 550b, etc.

11. Plato quotes both lines earlier at *Republic* 3, 390d.

12. For a detailed discussion of this point, see Chapter 4.

13. See *Iliad* 9.264 and 18.471.

CHAPTER 2 *Intimations of Immortality*

1. The myths are found in the conclusions to Plato's *Gorgias, Phaedo,* and *Republic,* and midway through the *Phaedrus*.

2. These lines left a strong mark on Plato, who drew on them in two of his dialogues (*Cratylus* 397d and *Republic* 469a).
3. Hesiod's myth of metals is sufficient to refute the once-fashionable notion that the idea of an afterlife was completely alien to Greece in the archaic period.
4. Some fifty years ago, in a Macedonian tomb were found the papyrus remains of an Orphic poem that treated the postmortem destiny of souls in a ritualistic context; see Betegh 2004. While work on this remarkable text is ongoing, the antiquity of the belief system that it records is quite certain.
5. See Clarke 1999, 305-12, for a detailed discussion.
6. The fragmentary verses of Empedocles are fully translated and discussed in Inwood 1992 and in McKirahan 2010.
7. Immortality in the sense of everlasting life is probably excluded because Empedocles's cosmology is cyclical, eternally alternating between a condition of perfect unity and a condition of multiplicity.
8. The fragmentary lines of Heraclitus are fully accessible in the books of Kahn 1979 and McKirahan 2010. Snell 1953 concludes his first chapter with an apt contrast between Homer and Heraclitus.
9. *Logos* in its early Greek usage straddles the meanings measure, numerical reckoning,

proportion, and story. Heraclitus uses the term to signify both his objective account of the world and the measures that make the world a cosmos, meaning an orderly structure. I discuss Plato's notion of reason, drawing on *logos* and related words in Chapter 4.

CHAPTER 3 *Bodies, Souls, and the Perils of Persuasion*

1. *Antidosis* 180.
2. My references to Socrates throughout this chapter refer to Plato's figure of that name. I make no assumptions about the historical accuracy of words Plato puts into the mouth of his Socrates character, except that I take the gist of Socrates's words in the *Apology* to be authentic. The historical Socrates has often been credited with advancing radical new ideas about the soul: see Robinson 1995, 3–4. Actually, however, much that Plato assigns to Socrates was already in the air during Socrates's youth, as we see from material presented in Chapter 2.
3. This dialogue has the name *Gorgias*.
4. The text is translated in Gagarin and Woodruff, 1995, 190–95.
5. I don't think this point has ever been given the emphasis it should receive.
6. Compare Plato, *Gorgias* 483c, spoken by Gorgias's defender Callicles: natural justice "shows that it

is right for the superior to have more than the inferior and the more powerful than the less powerful."
7. See Sextus Empiricus, *Against the Mathematicians* 7.73.
8. Gorgias wrote another work, *Concerning That Which Is Not*, in which he offers a systematic refutation of Parmenides's argument about that which exists and is true absolutely. See Gagarin and Woodruff 1995, 204-9. Parmenides himself had pilloried human opinion or judgment *(doxa)*. Gorgias went one better and turned Parmenides's argument against him.
9. Gagarin and Woodruff 1995, 198.
10. Especially by Callicles at 484c-486c.
11. *Protagoras* 313a-314b. This passage repeats and elaborates the contrasts drawn in the *Crito* between bodily health and moral health.
12. The word translated by moderation is *sophrosyne*, which is already found in its adjectival form in Homer. The etymology of *sophrosyne* is thinking *(phron)* safely *(sos)*. The quality that the term signifies (moderation, temperance, restraint) is of central importance in the fragments of Heraclitus and all Greek ethical texts.
13. See Plotinus, *Ennead* 1.4, where the ethical virtues are taken to be "purifications," as in *Phaedo* 69b, to prepare the soul for purely intellectual vision.

14. That impression is strongly reinforced by passages in such Platonic dialogues as the *Symposium, Republic,* and *Phaedrus.*
15. Aristotle, *On the Soul,* book 2.1.
16. See LS *Hellenistic Philosophers,* chapters 14 and 53.

CHAPTER 4 *The Politicized Soul and the Rule of Reason*

1. *Republic* 4.428d and 4.441e. I pass over the much-debated and troubling question of how or whether the tripartite state/individual analogy can fit the dialogue's assumption that the majority of persons lack the rational capacity to adequately exercise internal self-government.
2. The *Seventh Letter* attributed to Plato is probably not authentic, but its expression of Plato's disillusionment with Athenian politics rings completely true.
3. *Republic* 1.352d–e.
4. *Republic* 6,508e, and 7,517b.
5. For Plato's earlier treatment of this theme, see *Protagoras* 352b and *Euthydemus* 281a.
6. These actual facts of Greek politics are brilliantly described and analyzed in Thucydides's *History of the Peloponnesian War.*
7. *Republic* book 8.
8. Homer can register strong opposition to anarchy, as when Odysseus chides the commoner Thersites for speaking out of line, *Iliad* 2.246ff. This, however,

is a judgment that reflects the aristocratic values of the heroes rather than anything directly political in the sense of the common good.
9. *Republic* 4.437b.
10. "Some people [meaning the Stoics] say that passion is no different from reason, and that there is no dissension and conflict between the two, but a turning of the single reason in both directions, which we do not notice owing to the abruptness and speed of the change." Plutarch, *On Moral Virtue* 446f, translated in LS, *Hellenistic Philosophers* 65G.
11. This expression is excellently elucidated by M. Frede, 20-21.
12. *Republic* 4.440e.
13. *Republic* 8.550b.
14. *Republic* 9.588d.
15. *Republic* 9.586d-e.
16. *Republic* 10.611e.
17. *Phaedrus* 246a.
18. *Phaedo* 115c1. Socrates's identification of himself with his soon-to-be-disembodied soul is exactly antithetical to the Homeric notion that the corpse is the locus of a deceased human identity.
19. "Contemplative," the conventional translation of *theoretikos,* has nothing to do with meditation as it is practiced in religious rituals. What Aristotle supremely values is scientific understanding for

its own sake, or what we mean by "pure" when we speak of "pure," as distinct from "applied," mathematics.
20. *Timaeus* 41b.

CHAPTER 5 *Rationality, Divinity, Happiness, Autonomy*

1. In all three philosophies the heavenly bodies, thanks to their longevity and harmonious motions, are taken to be divine.
2. Divinity could even be applied to inanimate things. Thus Plato calls the Forms—the perfect, changeless, eternal paradigms of justice, beauty, and so forth—divine (*Phaedo* 80a).
3. For details, see the texts collected in LS *Hellenistic Philosophers*, chapter 23.
4. Catastrophic change of fortune, as exemplified by the fate of Oedipus, was acutely perceived by Aristotle to be the essence of Greek tragedy. In Sophocles's play *Oedipus Tyrannos*, the Chorus, having witnessed the downfall of Oedipus, question whether any human being could achieve more than "a semblance" of transitory *eudaimonia*. Such pessimism gave rise to the notion that no one should be deemed happy before the end of life.
5. See McKirahan (2010), text 10.121, 124. Another fragmentary line, from a lost play by Euripides, runs: "The *nous* belonging to us is in each person

a god," quoted by Cicero, *Tusculan Disputations* 1.65.
6. *Timaeus* 30a ff.
7. There are obvious affinities to the creation story in the first chapter of *Genesis,* where, at the end of each day God reviews his creative acts and sees that they are good.
8. For evidence and discussion, see McKirahan (2010), chapter 13.
9. *Metaphysics* 12, 1072b15. In his work *On the Parts of Animals* (686a26), Aristotle writes: "Of all animals man alone stands erect, in accordance with his godlike nature and substance. For it is the function of the godlike to think and to be wise."
10. Lucretius, in his great Epicurean epic, *On the Nature of Things,* makes constant appeal to reason *(ratio),* treating it as humanity's antidote to anxiety and superstition, and the source of Epicurus's liberating and salvific philosophy.
11. LS *Hellenistic Philosophers* 22E.
12. For a more detailed account composed for the general reader, see Long (1986), 147–58, 179–84.
13. LS *Hellenistic Philosophers* 54T.
14. I have emphasized these words because, as we shall see, they express central features of Stoic rationality and its empirical foundations.

15. Epictetus, *Discourse* 1.14. I draw on my translation in Long (2002), 25–6.
16. See Graver (2003), who writes, 348: "For Epictetus the entire point and purpose of Zeus-talk is to remind humans that we are not alone, that our reasoning powers have an analogue in, in fact are derived from, the order of the cosmos. Rationality itself, with all its perils and its dizzying possibilities, is his theme; if he speaks also of god as "father" (1.3), it is because our human potential is fulfilled only when we have come to see ourselves as akin to Universal Reason. The cosmic perspective gives us access to our own personhood."
17. "Study" is how I translate *theorei*, which is the same verb that Aristotle uses to categorize the "contemplative" role of reason (see Chapter 4). Epictetus repeats the word where he states that "the goal of human beings is contemplation *(theoria)*, self-conscious understanding *(parakolouthesis)*, and a lifestyle that is harmonious with nature." (1. 6.21)
18. *Gorgias* 501c. It has not been generally noted that Epicurus, writing a decade or so before Zeno, uses the verb *synkatatihesthai* in a similar way, fragment 29 Bailey.
19. *Apology* 38a, quoted by Epictetus in *Discourse* 1.26.18.

20. *Academica* 1.40, LS *Hellenistic Philosophers* 40B.
21. There is a vast modern literature on this topic; see especially Bobzien (1998).

Epilogue

1. I quote a slightly modified version of the recent translation by C. Gill, *Marcus Aurelius: Meditations, Books 1–6* (Oxford, 2013). His book should be consulted for its excellent treatment of the emperor's philosophy. I have discussed Marcus's treatment of "the self in the *Meditations*" in M. van Ackeren, ed., *A Companion to Marcus Aurelius* (Oxford, 2012), 465–80.

INDEX

Achilles, 17, 23, 25, 29, 32, 35, 45, 52, 53–54, 57, 73, 75, 143, 145
Aeschylus, 30
afterlife, 30, 56, 61–62, 68–69, 73, 75, 84, 91–92, 97, 117, 126, 151, 165–166, 210n
agency, 39, 169, 177, 192–193
analogy, of body and soul, 96, 106, 108, 110, 114; of city and soul, 44, 127–129, 149, 213n
Anaxagoras, 171–172
anger, 23, 39, 59, 136, 142, 143
animals, 40, 41, 63, 68, 78, 85, 144, 151–152, 185–187, 191, 216n

appetite(s), 39, 45, 112–113, 115, 122, 128, 135, 139–140, 144, 147–148, 149, 151, 153–154, 199
Aristotle, 3, 11, 12, 13, 21, 24, 28, 122–123, 155–159, 162, 164, 173, 176, 181, 182, 186
askesis, 110
assent, 179, 184, 188–192, 195
athletics, 109–110
autonomy, 12, 44, 83, 105, 110, 116, 140–141, 177–178, 188, 192, 194–195, 199

beauty, 10, 51, 99, 100, 102, 109, 151, 152, 185, 193

INDEX

blood, 54, 55, 121
body, 1, 5–6, 8–10, 13, 16–19, 23–26, 28–31, 33, 37–38, 42, 45, 51, 53, 56, 68, 69, 74, 79, 81, 83, 85, 108, 113, 115, 158, 179, 183; distinguished from soul, 88–90, 91, 92, 95, 96, 99–103, 125; Gorgias on, 99–105; Homeric notions of, 5–6, 25–26; negative value of, 118; subordination of, 88–90, 95–96, 100, 106, 109, 113, 117–118, 120, 122–123, 130–131, 149, 152–153, 167, 179, 183–184
brain, 1, 4, 24, 48, 207n
breath, 22, 23, 34–36, 38, 53, 74, 90–91

causality, 169–170, 173, 175, 177, 187–188, 192
Christianity, 46, 56, 163
Chrysippus, 176, 178
Cicero, 174, 188n, 190
Clarke, M., 37–38, 48

consciousness, 1, 15, 24, 26, 37–38, 147, 149, 152, 181, 188
contemplation, 15, 85, 156, 157, 173, 214n, 217n
corpse, 18, 23, 53, 57, 81, 83, 85, 91, 214n
cosmology, 45, 84, 154, 170–171, 175–176, 181
creationism, 163, 170, 172–173, 175
Cronus, 60, 72, 77

daimon, 8, 61, 76–80, 82, 97, 154, 166–168, 179–180, 182, 183, 188, 200
death, 7–8, 17–18, 23, 25, 31, 51–54, 56, 58, 60, 64, 74, 81, 82, 85, 91, 92, 95, 113, 117
deliberation, 40, 89, 111, 131–132, 141, 173
Demiurge of Plato, 156, 164, 170, 175
democracy, 98, 130, 134–135
Descartes, R., 48

INDEX

desire(s), 39, 102, 112, 114, 118–120, 121, 128, 134, 136, 138–141, 147, 148, 149, 151, 158, 167, 173, 192, 194, 200; of reason, 39, 140–141, 150, 186

determinism, 176, 192–193

developmental outlook, 2–3

divinity, 8, 11–12, 56, 66, 70, 77, 117, 154–157, 159, 162–164, 167, 171, 174–175, 177, 182, 183, 186, 194–195

doxai, 102–103, 106

dualism of mind/soul and body, 5, 7, 10, 15–18, 30, 38, 46, 48, 83, 97, 119, 121, 123, 125, 148–149

eidolon, 54, 92

Elysium, 58, 61–62, 68, 73, 75

emotion(s), 4, 32, 35–37, 39, 42–43, 103, 132, 142–145, 149, 158, 162, 187, 191

Empedocles, 8, 70, 76–80, 82, 85, 97, 113

Epictetus, 12, 178–186, 189, 193–194

Epicurus/Epicureanism, 12, 13, 26, 159, 163, 165, 173–174

erotic attraction, 100, 102, 130, 150, 152

etor, 35–36

eudaimonia, 154, 166–167, 182, 215n

fallible opinion, 102–103, 106–107

fire, 84

freedom, 93, 96, 112, 185

Gilgamesh, 59, 63

god(s), 17, 20, 51–52, 56–57, 59, 60, 64–66, 76, 77, 84, 145, 157, 164–165, 166, 169, 174, 208n; of Aristotle, 164, 166, 173; likeness to, 52, 60, 163–164; of Stoicism, 175–186

goodness, 95, 108, 109, 112, 131, 132, 137, 140, 141, 148,

INDEX

goodness *(continued)*
149, 151, 159, 170-171, 186, 199
Gorgias, 9-10, 93, 95-106, 212

Hades, 18, 23, 25, 58, 62, 70-71, 74, 75, 92, 97
happiness, 12, 51, 61-62, 65, 67-68, 71-73, 79, 95, 112, 115, 123, 132, 138, 154, 156, 159, 162-163, 165-169, 173-174, 193, 195
harmony, 84, 114, 133, 146-147, 170-171
health, 107-110, 114
heart, 6, 22, 26-27, 35-36, 41-42, 48, 90, 207n
Hebrew Bible, 59, 63-64
Hegel, G.F., 2
Helen of Sparta/Troy, 10, 58, 61, 66, 99-102
Heraclitus, 8, 11, 81-85, 113, 133, 159, 167
Hercules, 20
Herodotus, 103-104
Hesiod, 7, 58-67, 72, 73, 82, 85, 209
Homer, 3-7, 16-61, 70, 80, 81, 90, 103, 110, 121, 135-136, 142-146, 153, 165, 169, 198-199; psychosomatic holism of, 37-42, 90, 153. *See also* mind; soul
honor, love of, 143-144, 148
human dignity, 169, 196
human identity/nature, 1, 3, 6, 8, 15, 24-25, 29, 44, 46, 55, 56, 59, 67, 69, 78-79, 88-89, 91, 105, 118, 121, 123, 125-126, 138, 150-151, 153-154, 157, 163, 176-177, 182, 184-185, 192-193
Hume, D., 138

immortality, 7, 16, 17, 19-20, 30, 31, 46, 51-52, 56, 60, 64, 68-69, 71, 75, 79-80, 82, 85, 117-118, 153, 154, 156-157, 165, 198, 199
impressions, 179, 184, 186, 189, 190-191, 193-194
impulse(s), 40, 41, 45, 103, 136, 186, 190-191

INDEX

integrity, 94, 199–200
intellect, 26, 45, 60, 89, 122, 156–157, 158, 159, 163, 164, 167, 171, 172, 181, 198. See also *nous*
irrationality, 13, 40, 139, 187
Isles of the Blessed. *See* Elysium
Isocrates, 88–90, 91, 92, 96, 100, 105, 131

justice, 57–58, 60, 62–63, 64, 66, 67, 68, 72, 92, 93, 96, 106–107, 108–109, 114, 120, 131, 134, 146, 152, 167, 211–212nn

knowledge, 51, 64, 107, 113, 119–120, 130, 133, 149, 155, 190
kradie, 35, 40–42

life, 8, 15, 16, 18, 22–24, 25, 28, 29, 31, 33, 52, 58–59, 67, 78–79, 82, 85, 91, 108, 113, 131, 153, 156, 166, 200
logistikon faculty, 43, 128, 129, 139–140, 168
logos, 44, 83, 84, 99, 101, 133, 210n. *See also* reason

Marcus Aurelius, 199–200
mathematics, 16, 132–133, 156, 170
matter, 122, 171, 175
menos, 32–33
mental conflict, 39–42, 136, 138–139, 142, 152
metaphors of mind/soul, 89, 105–106, 130, 134, 136–137, 144, 146, 150–152, 156, 198
metaphysics, 149–150
mind: concepts of, 1–4, 8, 11, 13, 19–21, 24, 27, 33, 38, 46–48, 53, 85, 90, 104, 149, 172, 178, 182, 183, 186, 189, 193, 194–195; cardiovascular model of, 4–5; "commanding faculty" of, 187;

INDEX

mind *(continued)*
distinguished from body, 5-9, 28-30, 37, 88-89, 95-96, 120, 179; distinguished from matter, 171; Homeric words for, 26, 32-37; Stoic model of, 186-193; life of, 162, 168; unity of, 187. *See also* dualism of mind/soul and body

moderation, 93, 114, 141

monotheism, 163-164, 180

morality, 57-58, 62-64, 66-67, 72-73, 76, 80, 97, 107, 109, 158

mortality, 17, 31-32, 52-53, 56, 63, 66, 70, 82, 153-154, 156, 157, 165, 169, 208n

motivation, 13, 129, 140-141, 143, 150, 170, 187-188

myth(s), 54, 60, 63, 70, 85, 91, 95, 97, 99, 117, 126, 151, 157, 164, 166, 172, 209n

nature, life in agreement with, 163, 177

Nietzsche, F., 57

nous, 26, 60, 103, 156, 172, 209n, 216n

Odysseus, 17, 19, 29, 40-42, 45, 53, 54, 59, 83, 136

oligarchy, 134-135

Orphism, 69, 210n

pantheism, 175, 178

Parmenides, 212n

pathos, 31, 52, 85

perfection, 109, 146, 163, 164, 181, 199

phantasia, 187-188, 190, 193-194

philosopher contrasted with ordinary people, 118-122

philosopher rulers, 43, 130, 132, 147, 150, 155

philosophy: history of, 2; contrasted with rhetoric, 95-96, 116; and death, 113

phren, phrenes, 26, 35-36, 41-42, 54, 70, 103, 209n

INDEX

Pindar, 7-8, 70-76, 78, 80, 82, 83, 85, 95
Plato, 3-4, 7, 9-12, 21, 25, 29-31, 37, 39-48, 54-56, 64, 67, 74, 81, 83, 88-90, 93-98, 100, 105-123, 125-156, 162, 163, 167-168, 170-172, 181-182, 186, 198-199; *Apology,* 93-95, 108, 167; *Crito,* 106-108; *Gorgias,* 93, 95-97, 114, 116, 125-126, 147, 189; influence of, 118, 123; *Phaedo,* 113, 116-122, 125-126, 128, 140, 150, 152-153; *Phaedrus,* 150-151; *Protagoras,* 111; *Republic,* 126-150, 158; *Timaeus,* 154-155, 156, 167-168. *See also* soul
Platonism/Platonists, 7, 13, 18, 46-47, 51, 55-56, 122, 159, 166, 168, 176, 183
pleasure, 102, 105, 106, 113, 119, 123, 140, 144, 147-148, 174
Plotinus, 4, 15-18, 25, 46, 48, 121, 150, 159
politics, 11, 44, 89, 93, 98, 126-128, 129, 133-135, 140-141, 147, 155, 172
power(s), 10, 51, 52, 57, 93, 96, 100-102, 115, 134, 165, 169, 172, 173, 178, 181
prohairesis, 185
Prometheus, 59, 60, 64
prosperity. *See* happiness
Protagoras, 111
psyche, 6, 8, 17-18, 23-25, 28-31, 39, 41, 53-55, 59, 70-75, 79, 83, 88, 90-92, 95, 99, 103, 107-108, 142, 151-152, 208-209nn
psychosomatic holism, 32, 37-42, 153
Pyrrho, 22
Pythagoras, 21, 68-69, 76-77, 81, 97, 113, 133

rationality, 11-12, 13, 42-43, 84, 94, 103, 104, 119, 130, 132, 137-138, 147, 156-157, 158, 163, 168-169, 180, 182, 199

reason, 11, 39-41, 43, 45, 93,
    128, 130, 132-133, 136, 140,
    147, 149, 152, 159, 162, 168,
    169, 171, 172, 174-175,
    188; Aristotle on,
    156-158; contrasted with
    perception, 119; desires
    of, 39, 140, 150, 186; rule
    of, 122, 129-136, 141,
    143-152, 154-156, 169, 178,
    198-199, 199; Stoicism
    on, 163, 174-175, 178,
    182, 185, 194. See also
    logos
rhetoric, 9-10, 93-96,
    98-99, 101, 105, 107, 110,
    112-113, 115, 120, 125
rule, 130, 136-137, 141, 152.
    See also reason
Ryle, G., 48-49

self, 1-3, 8, 11, 18-20, 28, 32,
    38, 47, 59, 71, 74, 80-82,
    91-92, 118, 165, 178, 182,
    184-185, 188-189, 194,
    199; as divided, 42, 139,
    141, 152; as essentially
    intellectual, 15-16, 118,
    155
self-control, 9, 41, 105-106,
    112, 115, 162, 212n
self-perception, 188
sense perception, 119-120,
    183, 187, 190-191
shades, 52-55, 65, 70, 74, 81,
    83, 92, 95
shame, 39, 143
Snell, B., 29-30, 48,
    209n
Socrates, 9, 10, 24, 67-68,
    90, 93-95, 100, 107, 109,
    111-112, 133, 159, 167,
    189-190, 211n; trial and
    death of, 93-95, 116, 125,
    130, 152-153, 167, 195
soma, 8, 23, 25, 29, 88, 91, 99,
    101, 113, 209n
sophists, 96, 98, 111
Sophocles, 30
Sophrosyne, 212n
soul, 5-7, 9-10-13, 23-31, 35,
    37-40, 44, 45, 46, 55, 64,
    67, 68, 71, 74, 83-84, 113,
    120, 165; Aristotle's
    division of, 157-159; as

physical structure of, 26, 123, 183; authority over body, 88-90, 95-96, 100, 106, 109, 113, 117-118, 120, 122-123, 130-131, 149, 152-153, 183-184; distinguished from body, 88-90, 91, 92, 95, 96, 99-103, 125; goodness of, 94-95, 123, 140; Gorgias on, 99-105; health of, 107-110, 114; Homeric notions of, 25, 36-39; of the world, 170; Plato's tripartite division of, 10, 39-45, 128-129, 138-149, 151, 153; self-governing model of, 140; Stoic concept of, 89, 183; subordination of body to spirit, 16, 19, 24, 48, 55, 56, 61, 122, 128. See also *thumos; daimon*

Stoicism/Stoics, 12, 13, 19, 21-22, 26, 89, 139, 159, 162-165, 172-173, 174-196, 199-200

sublime, Plato's notion of, 154
synkatathesis, 189

techne, 133
teleology, 158-159, 169, 172-173
Thucydides, 103
thumos, 26, 33-45, 53, 59, 70, 74, 103, 142-145; as part of the soul, 41-44, 128, 141-145, 148, 151, 153, 209n
tranquility, 163, 173, 185
transmigration of souls, 68-69, 76-80, 97, 151
truth(s), 16, 98, 102, 107, 119-120, 127, 133, 147, 148, 149, 151, 155, 183, 199
tyranny, 130, 135, 148, 151

value(s), 22-23, 89, 90, 100, 118, 120, 123, 155, 183
virtue(s), 67, 72, 95, 109, 110, 123, 127, 148, 150, 173, 212n
volition, 184-185, 189, 190-192, 194, 195

INDEX

Williams, B., 207n, 209n
wisdom, 71, 83, 94, 102, 130, 150, 163, 174

Xerxes, 104

Zeller, E., 2, 207n
Zeno, 189–192
Zeus, 20, 57, 58, 59–60, 63, 64, 72, 73, 164, 172; in Stoicism, 164–165, 175, 178, 182, 184–185

REVEALING ANTIQUITY

G. W. Bowersock, General Editor

1. *Dionysos at Large,* by Marcel Detienne, translated by Arthur Goldhammer
2. *Unruly Eloquence: Lucian and the Comedy of Traditions,* by R. Bracht Branham
3. *Greek Virginity,* by Giulia Sissa, translated by Arthur Goldhammer
4. *A Chronicle of the Last Pagans,* by Pierre Chuvin, translated by B. A. Archer
5. *The Orientalizing Revolution: Near Eastern Influence on Greek Culture in the Early Archaic Age,* by Walter Burkert, translated by Margaret E. Pinder and Walter Burkert
6. *Actors in the Audience: Theatricality and Doublespeak from Nero to Hadrian,* by Shadi Bartsch

7. *Prophets and Emperors: Human and Divine Authority from Augustus to Theodosius,* by David Potter
8. *Hypatia of Alexandria,* by Maria Dzielska, translated by F. Lyra
9. *The Craft of Zeus: Myths of Weaving and Fabric,* by John Scheid and Jesper Svenbro, translated by Carol Volk
10. *Magic in the Ancient World,* by Fritz Graf, translation by Franklin Philip
11. *Pompeii: Public and Private Life,* by Paul Zanker, translated by Deborah Lucas Schneider
12. *Kinship Diplomacy in the Ancient World,* by Christopher P. Jones
13. *The End of the Past: Ancient Rome and the Modern West,* by Aldo Schiavone, translated by Margery J. Schneider
14. *The Invention of Jane Harrison,* by Mary Beard
15. *Ruling the Later Roman Empire,* by Christopher Kelly
16. *Mosaics as History: The Near East from Late Antiquity to Islam,* by G. W. Bowersock
17. *Histoires Grecques: Snapshots from Antiquity,* by Maurice Sartre, translated by Catherine Porter

18. *New Heroes in Antiquity: From Achilles to Antinoos,* by Christopher P. Jones
19. *Spartacus,* by Aldo Schiavone, translated by Jeremy Carden
20. *From Shame to Sin: The Christian Transformation of Sexual Morality in Late Antiquity,* by Kyle Harper
21. *Public Spectacles in Roman and Late Antique Palestine,* by Zeev Weiss

www.ingramcontent.com/pod-product-compliance
Lightning Source LLC
Chambersburg PA
CBHW071357160426
42811CB00111B/2212/J